RIVER OF FAITH

A Historical Perspective of
the International Foundation for Ewha Womans University

RIVER OF FAITH

믿음의 강

A Historical Perspective of the International Foundation for Ewha Womans University

Chang Hyun Shin Geer

International Foundation for Ewha Womans University

RIVER OF FAITH

A Historical Perspective of the International Foundation for Ewha Womans University

Written by Chang Hyun Shin Geer

First published 12 September, 2012
by Ewha Womans University Press
52, Ewhayeodae-gil, Seodaemun-gu, Seoul, Korea 120-750
Tel.: 82-2-3277-2965 / 362-6076
Fax.: 82-2-312-4312
E-mail: press@ewha.ac.kr

ISBN 978-89-7300-957-2 03900
Price: 22,000 won

Dedicated to

Dr. Helen K. Kim
Dr. Betty S. Mitchell

Foreword

It was George Santayana who once wrote: "Those who forget the past are condemned to repeat it." With this wonderful review of the history and context for the International Foundation for Ewha Womans University, Chang Hyun Shin Geer has given us the gift of remembering.

We dare not forget the world into which Ewha Womans University was born and the challenges it had to meet. We must not forget the strong and visionary women who risked livelihood and reputation to initiate educational opportunities for women in the late 19th century. We shall not forget the struggles of the Korean nation itself to achieve freedom and autonomy.

The 21st century in which we live is inundated with information. Geer's historical perspective will allow all its readers to better understand not only history but what the University is now and what its graduates have and will become.

And we will not forget the need and the vision that gave birth to the International Foundation for Ewha Womans University. Dr. Helen Kim knew the long term needs of the University would have to be sustained by gifts large and small from beneficiaries of the University as well as family and friends who desired to ensure that women in Korea – and even now worldwide – would have the opportunity to learn, teach, do research, heal, dance, sing, preach, and so much more. The world without educated women would surely be crippled without the gifts each one brings.

I give thanks to God for Dr. Geer's lifetime of love for the University as well as her never-ending work to guarantee the health and future of the International Foundation. We are in her debt for the contribution she brings to our remembering so that the future of both University and Foundation can continue to flow like a river that brings abundant life.

Sharon Zimmerman Rader
President, International Foundation for Ewha Womans University

Contents

Preface

The creation and rise of Ewha Womans University in Seoul, Korea to become the largest women's university in the world is an inspiring story. It has a history that can be told in many ways. This historical perspective of the International Foundation for Ewha Womans University (IFEWU) was written with the goal of tracing the role of what was described as the "Woman's Work for Woman" movement in the late 19th century in North America that led to the creation and nurturing of Ewha Womans University. The International Foundation for Ewha Womans University, Inc., continues in the spirit of that movement as it serves in partnership with Ewha to enlighten, educate and empower women in Korea and worldwide.

The history of the Foundation can be described as a component of a river of faith. The purposes of this book are to share the story of compassion and dedication in a multi-generational faith journey that enabled Ewha to grow into one of Korea's premier universities, and to demonstrate that the International Foundation for Ewha Womans University continues to be a vibrant supporter of Ewha as it moves forward in the 21st century.

It had been my original intent to prepare a history that was essentially a comprehensive recording of the first 40 years of the International Foundation. This objective changed soon after I began searching the past. It became obvious that placing the International Foundation within the context of the religious and social movements to educate and liberate women, specifically as it related to the creation, development, and ongoing support of Ewha Womans University, merited closer examination. With this change, recounting the inner workings of the Foundation was selectively directed towards themes, events, and individuals intended to reveal the enduring qualities of the organization as a whole. This approach has been taken because the Foundation is much more than merely the sum of its actions and accomplishments.

This change in approach introduced limitations, so this story is presented as a historical perspective. This historical analysis necessarily introduces some level of subjectivity as it is seen through the eyes of an Ewha alumna beneficiary and Foundation participant. Also, numerous individuals who contributed to this *River of Faith* and certainly deserving of recognition are missing from the narrative. As well, not all Foundation accomplishments are mentioned. The author accepts responsibility for omissions as she sought to tell what she thought was a bigger story. Especially, she regrets missing those themes, events, and individuals that would make the story more complete and reflective of actual happenings. Generally, but not always, Korean names are written in English according to their use in Korean or North American contexts. Attempts have been made to follow the spelling of names as preferred by the individuals themselves or as the names appear in reference documentation. Titles of individuals, including those academically, honorifically, or organizationally conferred, are generally, but not always, employed after their receipt. The author apologizes for any inaccuracies or inappropriatenesses regarding names and titles.

I wish to express sincere appreciation to the many persons who helped me in my research for the publication. In particular, I owe deep gratitude to Bishop Sharon Zimmerman Rader who has been leading the Foundation in recent years as President, and Mrs. Ji-yei Song Park, Executive Director, for helping me to obtain documents needed for research and to check accuracy. I am also grateful to Bishop Ann B. Sherer-Simpson, Dr. Bumsun Lee, Dr. Hai Won Chang, Dr. Hwain Chang Lee, and Dr. Jong H. Lee who reviewed the book's preliminary manuscript. Especially helpful were detailed proofreadings of the manuscript's second draft by Bishop Rader and by long-time personal church friend Mrs. Ruth N. Forman which clearly evidenced their past teaching experiences.

Bishop Sherer-Simpson's encouragement to me to write the historical perspective was greatly valued. Dr. Bumsun Lee and Dr. Hai Won Chang were especially helpful as eyewitnesses to history, being major participants in the Ewha *River of Faith* even before the Foundation was formed and going on to serve the Foundation for over four decades. My utmost gratitude goes to Mr. Moon Pyo Hong for sharing documents and information about his assistance to Dr. Helen Kim and his 20 years of working for the Foundation.

My gratitude goes to Dr. Paik Eun-mi, Associate Vice President for Office Relations and Development and Professor of Division of Christian Studies, and Researcher Son Hyun-ji, Ewha Archives, of Ewha Womans University for their assistance in acquiring materials for this publication. A special note of gratitude goes to Ewha Womans University Press for its impeccable preparation of the book for publication.

I am especially grateful to my husband, Prof. Ira W. Geer, for his encouragement and helpful suggestions.

Chang Hyun Shin Geer, Ph.D.

Prologue

"You are making a great mistake. Why don't you work the other way?" said an intelligent Korean man to a missionary. "If you want to win Korea, win the women. Win the mothers, and all Korea will be Christian." But they cannot be reached by men, and but a handful of women (including Mrs. Mary Scranton) who love Christ have gone to seek them.

Mrs. Scranton, recognizing the necessity for a home where she could gather the women about her, wrote to the Society for permission to buy a piece of property in a commanding situation, overlooking the American Legation. ... (on) October 23, 1885, the Woman's Foreign Missionary Society was the owner of real estate in the city of Seoul, and the work of educating the women and girls was begun. ...

... soon after the new building was occupied, the president of the (Korean) Foreign Office, in order to show the people that Mrs. Scranton had the confidence of the Government, sent the school name, "Pear Flower School," which was framed according to custom, and hung over the big gate.

Frances J. Baker, *The Story of the Woman's Foreign Missionary Society of the Methodist Episcopal Church* (1896)[1]

With this, Ewha Haktang came into being.

Introduction

Many years later with a motto of "Earning Friends for Ewha," Ewha Womans University's first Korean President, Dr. Helen K. Kim, heralded a vision that was formalized shortly after her death in 1970 as a sharing partnership through the establishment of the International Foundation for Ewha Womans University. The creation of the Foundation consummated a long-building manifestation of pure compassionate human spirit of shared friendships embedded in missionary endeavors. Tracing the origins and history of the International Foundation for Ewha Womans University is inherently fascinating. It is a case study from global history during the late 19th century to the 21st century when Korea moved from an impoverished tradition-bound society holding females in very low regard to modern status. It tells of Methodist women's foreign mission "for their sisters across the sea," with the assistance of individuals, like-minded groups, alumnae and friends of Ewha Womans University that clearly succeeded in helping grow educational opportunities for women in Korea. Established as an international organization centered in North America, the Foundation has been instrumental in carrying on and strengthening these long-term efforts directed towards promoting the education and liberation of women in Korea through what started as the Pear Flower School, Ewha Haktang.

The major goal of the Foundation has been to assist Ewha Womans University as it works towards creating an environment in which women are respected as rational human beings functioning fully in society. The effort to lend support to the aspirations of women in Korea to become educated and valued has been neither rapid nor easy. It is a story well over a century in length along a path strewn with numerous obstacles. Individuals, groups and organizations persevered, making their contributions to the cause of educating women, as generations passed and Ewha emerged. Conditions and needs have changed with the flow of history, but the loyalty of friends and graduates of the University assured and continue to affirm ongoing support.

Modestly beginning as a Methodist missionary school in 1886 with one girl, Ewha grew into a premier institution of higher education with over 21,200 women students enrolled at undergraduate and graduate levels in 2010. Since its beginning through 2010, Ewha graduated 188,420 women (and is adding more than 5,200 alumnae each year) embodied with Christian ethics, education and skills that have empowered them to apply their human talents and values while benefiting the larger society. In order to grow such an outstanding institution that achieves these goals, many individuals toiled for generations during extremely difficult periods of social, political, and economic turmoil, and awakening. Most, particularly those long gone, could not have dreamed of what their efforts would produce. Although they did not know where it would flow, they surely knew their actions were adding to a growing *River of Faith*.

Part 1

Woman's Work for Woman

Woman's Work for Woman, a novel missionary movement launched in the latter part of the 19th century in the Northeastern U.S., played an instrumental role in the education of women far beyond North America. This broad-based movement sponsored women missionaries who traveled to many regions around the world.

The establishment and evolution of Ewha is closely tied to the women's mission movement conceived, established, conducted, and financed by women. The movement legitimatized the ministry abroad of single women who were attracted to educational work as the key to social advancement for women.

The beginnings of the *Woman's Work for Woman* movement started modestly in 1869 by the founding of the Woman's Foreign Missionary Society (WFMS) of the Methodist Episcopal Church. The aim was to have women more fully participate in foreign mission by reaching into every church and enlisting every woman in every church as a member. Life was given to the movement by having every Christian woman lay aside two cents a week as membership dues. The amount was so small

1895 photograph of the founders of Woman's Foreign Missionary Society [Frances J. Baker] [2]

that all women, even the most humble, could have a share in pursuing the work and raising funds. This was called an *organization of the littles* that produced a full and steady stream of donations.[3]

This movement made possible the networking and ideology of mission work by women for women. It laid the foundation that resulted in the Woman's Foreign Missionary Society sponsoring women missionaries who, beginning in 1869, set out for countries including India, China, Japan, and Korea. Missionaries from the Society opened the first schools and colleges for girls and women in India, China, and Korea. In general, it was the funds from the Mission Board of the Woman's Foreign Missionary Society which supported the missionaries and the necessary educational facilities.

The Woman's Foreign Missionary Society was formed in Boston, Massachusetts by a handful of women on a stormy night on March 23, 1869 at the Tremont Methodist Episcopal Church. WFMS was essentially an independent organization which was operated and managed by women for the expressed purpose of sending women missionaries abroad. Isabella Thoburn and Clara Swain were sent to India as the Society's first missionaries. Women's mission work had developed into a dominant force in Protestant mission activity and became labeled with the slogan, *Woman's Work for Woman*. This elevated women Christian missionaries to work comparable to preaching by men ministers. The slogan had powerful impact on generating adequate financial support. It and the large membership of women with a sense of ownership of its entire operation from beginning to end made it possible to establish and operate hospitals, schools and orphanages in many places of great need.[4]

Education for Girls and Women in Korea

In 1885, Mrs. Mary F. Scranton, destined to become the first Principal of Ewha Haktang, arrived in Korea under the sponsorship of the WFMS. She was followed by a stream of women missionaries over many decades, including Miss Lulu E. Frey and Miss Alice R. Appenzeller. The origins of Ewha Womans University can be traced back to these early missionaries provided by WFMS. It is probably safe to say that the "Womans" term in Ewha's name can be considered as both a recognition and celebration of the WFMS "Woman's Work for Woman" movement that led to the University's beginnings.

By the mid-19th century, support of missions had become a popular way of sanctifying American democracy and way of life. Foreign mission efforts helped give a religious authenticity to American culture. Education was becoming a major driving force of missions abroad. American missionaries carried the gospel of education to the farthest corners of the world. John Franklin Goucher was an example. He was a Methodist minister from Pennsylvania who took educational mission to Asia. He went to Japan, Korea, India, and China in the latter part of the 19th century to help set up mission schools and hospitals. In Korea, Dr. Goucher

Mrs. Mary F. Scranton, 1st Principal of Ewha
[Ewha Archives]

persuaded the government to allow foreigners to establish a mission. Subsequently, he helped to organize hospitals and schools. He encouraged Mrs. Mary Scranton in the mid-1880s to go to Korea as a missionary to open a school for girls. He and his wife provided financial support for the endeavor. It is interesting to note that at about the same time, he founded a college of education for women in 1885 in Baltimore, Maryland (later to become Goucher College). Dr. Goucher played a continuing role behind the scenes in Korean mission work. Decades after helping to establish Ewha Haktang, he sent $2,000 to inspire Principal Lulu E. Frey who worked to register Ewha as a college with the Japanese Colonial Government in control of Korea at the time.[5]

The zeal of mission among North Americans opened a frontier for women in Korea. Korea was faced with constraining hardships under Japanese domination and then colonial rule while the traditional societal bondage of women was the continuing norm. The Japanese colonial educational policy for Koreans after the annexation of Korea in 1910 was aimed at teaching minimum skills for clerical levels. Higher education was not intended for Koreans and higher education for women was disallowed. Traditional Korean social norms regarding the education of women were simultaneously severely limiting. The vision of education for women as brought by American missionaries was revolutionary in the Korean context. The education of women was a huge challenge, which at the same time required additional support because of the growing demand by increasing numbers of girls and women seeking educational opportunities.[6]

Korea in the mid-19th century and later was marked by the geopolitical complexity of Confucian traditionalism, foreign policies of Korea, Japan and the U.S., and pervasive economic poverty. Korean women and girls were harshly treated:

> *Family life is thoroughly patriarchal. Marriage is almost obligatory; the unmarried state a shame to either sex. Male children are esteemed because they perpetuate the ancestral line and maintain ancestral worship. Female children, at marriage, are transferred to the family of their husbands, and therefore, are lightly esteemed by their parents; while the wife who brings forth only daughters is likely to find herself soon replaced in her spouse's affections. Young people take no part in the choice of their partners. Women of the better classes rarely leave their homes. Those seen upon the streets all belong to the lower orders. The wife is never looked upon as a companion by her helpmeet, and if she belongs to a respectable class, passes her life in the seclusion of the woman's quarters.*[7]

The American women missionaries confronted the challenges they faced with tenacious faith in order to serve and save "heathen" women. The ultimate goal of missions was to evangelize the women and men in preparation for the second coming of Jesus. Along with Christianizing women, there were the strong undercurrents of educating and serving the ignored women to uplift their humanity.[8]

The crucial role that the WFMS played in the financial support for what was to become Ewha Womans University cannot be overstated. The WFMS sent women missionaries to Korea while providing funds for expenses, salaries of teachers, doctors, and buildings. Back in the U.S., the membership dues and donations to WFMS were carefully managed and invested to provide continuing support decade after decade.

Ewha Haktang, started by Mrs. Mary Scranton, radiated the light that started a new beginning for women in Korea. Extraordinary accomplishments were made through steady, patient work by a stream of committed Christian individuals. Miss Louise Christina Rothweiler succeeded Scranton as the next Principal in 1890. She served for two years. In 1892, Ewha welcomed a new Principal, Miss Josephine O. Paine, who served for 15 years.

The early 20th century marked a transformational period of progress in achieving modern higher education opportunities for Korean women. This period of innovation was started in 1910 by Miss Lulu E. Frey, the fourth Principal of Ewha.

Lulu E. Frey was born in 1868 in Sydney, Ohio. She decided to become a missionary in 1889. After graduation from Ohio Wesleyan University, she was appointed in 1893 by the Cincinnati Woman's Foreign Missionary Society as a missionary to Korea. She served as the Ewha Principal from 1907 to 1921. She wished to establish a college for the increasing female student population. In 1910, Miss Frey made a critical first step for Korean women by officially registering a college for Ewha Haktang graduates. She was the Principal of Ewha Haktang during a politically tumultuous period in Korea when colonial domination by Japan was being implemented, but she succeeded in laying the cornerstone of her dream to educate Korean women to the highest level. The financial support to fulfill that educational goal was provided by gifts from the WFMS and individuals, including Dr. and Mrs. Henry Goucher.

Miss Lulu E. Frey, 4th Principal of Ewha [Ewha Archives]

From the time of the 1910 annexation of Korea by Japan, Koreans sought higher education as part of their determined drive for independence. With the change of policy by Japan after the 1919 March First Movement uprising for national survival, Koreans were given access to higher education. The Japanese colonial policy of Rule by Bayonet (Budan Tochi) that had prevailed for a decade was changed to Culture Administration through Appeasement by Japanese Governor-General Saito Minoru. American missionaries who witnessed the growing aspiration helped to promote the educational opportunity for Koreans.

During the turmoil of their Independence Movement against Japanese colonial power, Koreans saw that education was one of the empowering avenues for young Korean people. Keijo Imperial University (later, Seoul National University), Chosun Christian College (later, Yonsei University), Bosung College (later, Korea University), and other higher educational institutions were established for men while Ewha College was the only institution started for women. Education was one of the key avenues for Koreans seeking nationalism and independence.[9]

Miss Frey, who was described as having the heart of a Korean, believed passionately in the need for educating Korean women. She conceived the idea of Ewha as a college and registered Ewha Haktang as a college separate from Ewha primary and secondary school levels. She fervently believed in equal treatment and high standards in education for women. Under her guidance over a decade, the Ewha college program grew in both breadth and depth. In August 1919, after ordeals of protecting Ewha students involved in the March First Independence Movement, she returned to the U.S. for a furlough and much needed rest. On March 18, 1921, she died in a Boston hospital. She was 53 years old. She did not live to see her vision realized of a college campus for Korean women. One of the students who Miss Frey had educated and mentored was Helen K. Kim, destined to become the first Korean president of Ewha in 1939.

Miss Jeannette Walter and two other teachers came from the United

States in 1911. Professor Walter was educated in Baker and Northwestern Universities and earned her master's degree in higher education from the Graduate School of Education at Columbia University. She became a missionary through the Topeka branch of the Woman's Foreign Missionary Society. After Miss Frey's passing, Professor Walter served as the head of Ewha Haktang for one and one-half years before becoming Ewha's business manager.

Historical Context Surrounding Ewha in the Early 20th Century

The early 20th century brought Korea an extended period of political, educational and social turmoil and strife. The troubled state of national identity during the impact of Russo-Japanese War brought economic instability and loss of self-determination for Korea. In 1905, Japan imposed its rule by occupying Korea and declaring it as a protectorate.

The Korean educational system was determined by Japanese authority for the benefit of Japan. The Japanese colonial government established educational systems to meet its goals. Private schools for primary and secondary schools sprung up as Koreans tried to meet their own educational aspirations and societal needs while raising national identity.

Mission schools, as private institutions funded by foreign countries, were welcomed by Koreans, particularly for girls. Girls and women were not given opportunities to be educated in public schools.

The early 20th century was an awakening period for western countries seeking new economic opportunities in Asia. There was relentless aggression by the western nations to grow trade with China, Korea, Japan, India and other Asian nations. India and Sri Lanka were colonized by England, Indonesia by the Dutch, and The Philippines by the Americans. Korea was subjected to and overcome by aggressive Japan colonialism.

During the same time period, American missionaries plied Korea with Christianity and, with it, education. During such a difficult period, Koreans seeking change were receptive to the presence of American missionaries and what they brought with them.

Launching a New Campus: The Audacity of Alice R. Appenzeller

Miss Alice Rebecca Appenzeller assumed the presidency of Ewha College in 1922, the office she held until 1939. Among the many missionaries contributing to Ewha's development and growth, Miss Alice R. Appenzeller was perhaps the foremost in terms of the depth and length of her benevolence directed towards growing Ewha, especially when she was the president of the institution. In the 1930s, she directed her energy towards developing the networking essential for building a financial base for what was to become Ewha Womans University.

Alice R. Appenzeller, 6th President of Ewha College [Ewha Archives]

Alice Appenzeller was born in Seoul, Korea, on November 9, 1885. Her parents, Rev. and Mrs. Henry G. Appenzeller, arrived in Korea as the first Methodist missionary family to Korea on April 5, 1885. Miss Appenzeller was the first child of an American missionary family born in Korea. In 1885, Reverend Henry Appenzeller built the first Protestant church in Korea, Chung Dong First Methodist Church. He also built Bae Chai Middle and High School for boys. In July of 1902, Rev. Appenzeller tragically drowned trying to save others while on a trip to Mok Po by ship. Because of his death, the Appenzeller family returned to the U.S.

After the family's arrival in Lancaster, Pennsylvania, Alice Appenzeller enrolled in Miss Stahr's School for Girls. After graduation, she studied at Wellesley College in Massachusetts and attended a summer session at Harvard University. While she was a student of Wellesley College she sang in the choir, was active in volunteer activities, and developed an extensive network of friends. Her close friend was Jessie Wilson, the daughter of Woodrow Wilson (at the time President of Princeton University and later President of the United States). Miss Appenzeller was awarded a Bachelor's degree in 1909.

In 1914, she was appointed by the WFMS as a missionary to Ewha. Later, during her first furlough home, she attended Teachers College, Columbia University for graduate study and earned a M.A. degree in 1922. In the same year, she was elected as President of Ewha College. Later, in 1932, she was ordained by the Korean Methodist Church in Chung Dong First Methodist Church in Seoul.

Along with her spirituality and intellectual strengths, Miss Appenzeller's entrepreneurial skills were evident. In her 30th reunion yearbook she notes "A missionary's furlough is the time for promotion and cultivation of the home end, and each of my three holidays has been busy in that. Last time Wellesley President Caroline Hazard gave me $1,000 for our library fund ..."[10]

View of Sinchon land identified for the future Ewha campus [Ewha Archives]

It had been evident even before Miss Appenzeller became President of Ewha College that the college needed a new campus. Buildings which were shared with Ewha Primary, Junior and High Schools had become crowded because of increased enrollments. Miss Lulu E. Frey, in 1918, was instrumental in locating a future campus site for Ewha. Miss Frey had consulted with Dr. Goucher, who was then serving as a missionary from the Methodist Church in Baltimore, Maryland, to search for suitable campus land in Sinchon, in the outskirts of Seoul, for Ewha College. A tentative site was identified.

Accreditation of Ewha as a college gave rise to protracted challenges centering on financial need. The WFMS was the major outside source of financial support to run the college at the time, as was the support of the other parts of Ewha Haktang since its beginning. Ewha was also receiving some united support from the Methodist Episcopal Church South, the United Church of Canada, and the Australian Church. However, acquiring funds to purchase land and build a campus seemed by most to be an insurmountable goal.

Stone bench with inscription recognizing Mrs. Philip Hayward Gray [Ewha Archives]

It was Alice Appenzeller's dream to model Ewha College after her alma mater, Wellesley College, on a Sinchon campus. But a huge amount of funding had to be raised for purchasing lands and the construction of campus buildings. Such a dream in a country occupied by Japanese colonialists and experiencing economic, religious, and gender challenges for women surely was in need of a miracle. A woman of strong faith and exuberant character, Miss Appenzeller took steps to realize the dream.

In 1923, Mrs. Philip Hayward Gray from Detroit, Michigan was traveling in Korea with her two daughters. She visited Ewha College because of the guidance of a Canadian missionary, Miss Saxe. Miss Appenzeller, with much praying, showed the Gray family the land then on the outskirts of Seoul which was being sought as the site for a new Ewha College campus. Miss Appenzeller's prayers were soon answered when Mrs. Gray donated a gift of $30,000 towards purchasing 45 acres in Sinchon. Later, she contributed another $25,000 for the campus. Mrs. Gray asked that her name be left unknown. However, history notes that her name was inscribed on a marble stone bench near Pfeiffer Hall. The original inscription was removed by Japanese order, but was later re-inscribed by Ewha to honor the donations so critical to Ewha's future.

By 1926, the total student population on the existing Chung Dong campus, including primary, middle, high school and college, was 800. The 383 students of the college were severely hampered in their studies because of the lack of classrooms. It was very difficult to teach without sufficient facilities for laboratories and dormitories. The size and facilities of Chung Dong campus were simply not adequate to provide a viable learning environment. With the land now possessed in Sinchon, the focus turned to looking for resources to build a campus.

With the help of the Methodist Episcopal Church South and Methodist Episcopal Church of the United States, a committee was organized for Ewha College campus development. Fundraising for the construction of the Sinchon campus was carried out both in Korea and the United States. The Canadian Women's Missionary Society became involved and participated in assisting the construction of the buildings as well. The task for building the Ewha campus became an ecumenical and international endeavor.

In 1929, the Ewha Womans College Trustee Board concluded that it needed $900,000 to proceed with the development of the Sinchon campus. It was decided that $450,000 was to be raised from outside Korea and an equivalent amount was to be raised in Korea by the Ewha Trustee members. The trustee members consisted of both Americans and

Koreans. They were Bishop Herbert Welch, Miss Alice R. Appenzeller, Dr. Heung Woo Shin, Bishop Chang Woo Kim, Miss Jeannette Walter, and Miss Ada B. Hall.

The fundraising in the United States was an immense undertaking, as it coincided with the world economic downturn and the beginning of the Great Depression following the Stock Market Crash of 1929. President Appenzeller approached the U.S. fundraising in her usual fashion of relying on her own optimism and fervent prayers. She was a tall, confident, and articulate missionary who was up to the task.

With her unique background, born in Korea and educated in the United States, Ewha President Appenzeller marshaled all her resources, including a personal network, to seek funding. In fundraising, network building is most often the key to success. She was determined to raise the fund via WFMS and her friends through missionaries and the mission network. While the challenge was great to raise funds for the first institution of higher education for women in Korea, she was motivated by the knowledge that education is crucial to bringing about change in a needy tradition-bound society.

The fundraising in the United States at the time of economic depression must have seemed to be a fool's errand, although it was a seminal event in Ewha's history. In 1929, President Appenzeller traveled by ship and train to New York City where the WFMS office was located.

Later, at an Ewha alumnae meeting in 1931, Appenzeller delivered a speech about her experiences in fundraising, " ...When I was heading for the United States for fundraising it was an overpowering burden on me, and the excruciating stress compelled me to wish the ship would wreck before reaching harbor."[11] Her comments reflected the immobilizing stress she must have felt in attempting to raise an enormous amount for building a campus during a worldwide economic depression.

She set up a fundraising office at New York's 150th Street and 5th Avenue. She organized a fundraising Executive Committee with Mrs.

Francis J. McConnell as the Chair (wife of Bishop J. McConnell, President, Foreign Mission Board of the Methodist Church). The Committee Members were Mrs. Francis J. McConnell – Chair (WFMS), Miss Elizabeth R. Bender – (WFMS), Rev. Peong K. Yoon – (Minister of Korean Methodist Church), Miss Esther Case – (The Methodist Episcopal Church South, Mission Council Work), Miss Alice R. Appenzeller – (President, Ewha Womans College).

During her fundraising stay in New York, President Appenzeller made contact with Mr. and Mrs. Henry Pfeiffer. Mrs. Pfeiffer was President of the Woman's Home Missionary Society of New York. When she went to visit Mrs. Pfeiffer, who lived in a modest apartment, she prayed in the hallway of the building while waiting to see Mrs. Pfeiffer. Her fervent prayers were answered just they were when she had taken Mrs. Philip Hayward Gray and her daughters to see the Sinchon site. Mr. and Mrs. Pfeiffer agreed to contribute $50,000 towards the construction of the first building on the new campus. They continued to direct funds to Ewha over the years, and a total of $259,000 was given for Ewha building construction by 1940. Also, a Pfeiffer Endowment was funded that continues to support the maintenance of Pfeiffer Hall through the International Foundation for Ewha Womans University.

President Appenzeller returned to Korea in 1931 after energetically conducting two years of fundraising in the U.S. After returning from the U.S., she succumbed to a month-long hospitalization because of the exhaustion from fundraising. But the funds that Appenzeller brought in were enough to begin building a mecca for women's higher education in Korea. An extremely fortunate coincidence was that Korean money was devalued at the time, doubling the purchasing power of the contributed U.S. dollars. Appenzeller continued her fundraising efforts in the years to follow, corresponding with donors and friends in the U.S.

Because of the persistent fundraising campaign, funds were realized from sources in the United States and Korea for construction of the Sinchon campus. As already noted, the Pfeiffers supported the building of the first building on the campus. Continuing its long history of support for Ewha, WFMS pledged $60,000 towards the construction of the Sinchon campus. A sum of $20,000 was received from the Mission Board of the Methodist Episcopal Church South, another $10,000 from Edwin S. Emerson. Sixteen persons and churches including the First Methodist Episcopal Church, Lancaster, Pennsylvania each donated $1,000 or more as duly recorded in a 1935 Dedication Program. Twelve Americans donated through bequests for specific buildings. Forty-nine Koreans residing in Korea joined with contributions for building the Ewha campus.

President Appenzeller wrote on April 7, 1934 of *Dreams Coming True*. Excerpts from her writing follow:

> *Ever since 1918 when Dr. John F. Goucher first discovered the lovely valley at Sinchon where the new Ewha College buildings are rising, we have been dreaming of the new college. ...*
>
> *... Present and former teachers, many friends of the college, Korean, American and those of other nationalities have shown their interest by their gifts. Every brick and stone represents someone's loving thought and care. We cannot regard these buildings as merely material things. They truly represent spiritual values. ...*
>
> *We have been asked what plan we have for endowment, or how we expect to secure an income sufficient to allow us to move. We reply that the same method that has brought us these buildings – that is faith and prayer and work – will also provide the necessary income. We believe this thoroughly, but we know that it means hard, faithful work, much prayer and our best use of brain, heart and mind. We know that God has much more and better things in store for Korean womanhood, better educational opportunities and more openings for rich life than have ever been dreamed of yet. We believe that He is using Ewha College as an*

President Appenzeller laying cornerstone of first building on Sinchon campus [Ewha Archives]

> *instrument and we want most of all to be worthy of His trust. We appeal to everyone who reads these words, all friends of Ewha and of Korean womanhood to help us in this great undertaking.*[12]

President Appenzeller's comments eloquently stated that faith, prayer and work will provide what is necessary in the future. Indeed, the fund-raising and subsequent successes showed that efforts begun many decades earlier were gaining momentum. Remarkably, the multitudes of women who formed WFMS and donated two cents a week towards *Woman's Work for Woman* had been joined by others across the generations. To this day, each succeeding generation picked up where the previous one left off, made its contribution, and then passed the challenge on to the next. Confident that their work was worthwhile while not knowing where it would lead marks these efforts as true acts of faith.

The Pfeiffer Endowment

Perhaps the most critical work that President Appenzeller accomplished during her fundraising trip to New York was making the long-lasting connection between Mr. and Mrs. Henry Pfeiffer and Ewha.

Mr. Henry Pfeiffer (1857-1939) married Annie Merner (1860-1946), owned a wholesale drug business in St. Louis, Missouri, and founded the Pfeiffer Chemical Company. He had considerable business success which enabled the couple to engage in philanthropic causes under the auspices of the Methodist Episcopal Church, much of it through Mrs. Pfeiffer's work. After the couple moved to New York in 1927, Mrs. Pfeiffer became president of the Woman's Home Missionary Society (WHMS) of the New York Conference.

The Pfeiffers lived modestly and were childless. They contributed generous amounts of their earned fortune for gifts of buildings, cash, and stocks to institutions of higher education in the U.S. and around the world. Mrs. Pfeiffer received honorary degrees from eight institutions in the United States for her good works.

History records the contributions of the Pfeiffers among the most indispensable financial support given to Ewha because of their timeliness, amounts, and perpetuity. The funds contributed by the Pfeiffers have assisted Ewha since the early 1930s. Their legacy continues to assist Ewha in the form of endowments now carried out through the International Foundation. Pfeiffer Hall is the main administration building where the University president's office is located.

Mr. and Mrs. Henry Pfeiffer [Ewha Archives]

Pfeiffer Hall, first major building on Sinchon campus [Ewha Archives]

The Foundation manages the Pfeiffer Endowment for its maintenance. The value of the Pfeiffer Endowment in 2010 was $706,115.

"The Only College for Women in Korea Needs Your Help": Helen K. Kim

The passion of Alice Appenzeller to provide educational opportunities for Korean women through Ewha Womans College knew no bounds. This passion was equaled, if not surpassed, by Helen K. Kim. Both were visionaries who reached across national borders with the common goal of providing Korean women with the opportunity to acquire a first-class Christian-based college education.

Helen K. Kim was born on February 27, 1899 in Incheon, Korea, the fifth of eight children of Kim, Chi-yon and Park Dora. At the age of nine, Helen K. Kim was sent to Ewha Haktang in Seoul. In 1918, she was the first graduate of Ewha's three-year college preparatory department. She remained at Ewha and taught middle school students for four years. In 1921, she was sent to the United States for further education.

She first went to Wichita, Kansas where she stayed with the family of Miss Jeannette A. Walter, who had been a missionary from 1911 to 1926, including a 1.5-year tenure as principal of Ewha (1921-1922). Within a few days of arrival, she was struck by typhoid fever. She apparently had become infected during her ocean travel aboard a cargo ship. She was advised by the attending doctor to be hospitalized, but she made it clear that she strongly preferred to remain in the Walter home. She called Mr. and Mrs. Walter her parents. The Walters followed her wishes and kept her in their house, where she was cared for by the Walter family and friends. Helen Kim was deeply touched by the love and compassion she received, and referred to those who cared for her as her beloved American family. Through this experience, America became her second home.

After recovering from her illness, she attended Ohio Wesleyan University and then went on to Boston University. While studying at Boston University, in the Fall of 1923, she participated in the Woman's Mission Council meeting. There, she met Mrs. Evelyn Riley Nickolson, Chair, Executive Committee, WFMS, and appealed to her to organize an international Christian women's organization to promote peace and social justice along the lines of the League of Nations. The proposed Women's International Association would promote peace, professionalize the work of women, protect women and children, and establish justice. By 1929, Methodist women were ready to follow through on Helen Kim's vision and the Methodist Church created an international department.[13]

In 1930, she began her studies at Teachers College, Columbia University. She received a Ph.D. in education in 1931. While studying at Teachers College, she had engaged in fundraising on Ewha's behalf. Before she left for Korea, she was involved in the creation of a brochure for fundraising in association with Mrs. J. M. Avann, Executive Secretary of the Chicago, Illinois, WFMS Chapter. The message of the brochure conveyed was that "The Only College for Women in Korea Needs Your Help!"

President Alice Appenzeller and Dr. Helen Kim
[Ewha Archives]

She continued fundraising efforts after returning to Korea, where she had become Dean and Vice President of Ewha College. In November 1931, she sent a fundraising letter to the friends of Ewha College. The brochure developed with Mrs. Avann was included, which described Ewha College as the Woman's Christian College of Korea, its accomplishments from 1910 through 1931, and the financial needs for buildings, estimated to be $450,000. The brochure indicated that a gift of $1,000 would enable one to name a room. Her fundraising letter was as follows:

November 1931

Dear Friends,

Three months travel among American Christians convinced me again of their continued zeal to share the best in their lives with people of other lands. The expression of their devotion and interest makes it reasonable to believe that missions, or the interchange of good works, are to take on an increasing magnitude in the future. The discovery enables me to return home heartened and strengthened, ready to face the manifold problems connected with Ewha College, which is a living symbol of harmonious co-operation of the West and the East. A new feeling of assurance that friends in America will do their part in this joint project hastened me home with constituency to do its share. Allow me to take this opportunity to thank the friends who have already given and those who are going to respond generously as the "Depression" disappears. It is a joy to know you all. May God bless you!

Sincerely Yours,
Helen K. Kim, Dean, Ewha College.

Alice Appenzeller and Helen Kim diligently engaged in growing and nurturing networks of personal friends and friends for Ewha. They both were prolific correspondents who sought connections with others while always mindful of Ewha's needs. Alice R. Appenzeller wrote to college friends, missionary friends, and church friends. Helen Kim's letters were eloquent articulations with the many friends she met in the United States and in her travels.

Ewha's 50th Anniversary Celebration - *River of Faith*: 1936

In 1930, the Methodist Episcopal Church, the Mission Board of the Methodist Episcopal Church South, and the United Church of Canada jointly formed a Cooperating Board for Ewha. In the several years following, Pfeiffer Hall, Case Music Hall, Emerson Chapel, and Thomas Gymnasium buildings were all built with outside financial assistance, which included funds from the Cincinnati Chapter of WFMS and the Australian Church. The dormitory building, with an additional donation from Mr. and Mrs. Pfeiffer and the help of the Canadian Missionary Society and the WFMS, was begun in 1934. The Kindergarten Building (Clara Hall, The Education Building) was started with American children's offerings through the WFMS.

On March 9, 1935, on the birthday of Lulu E. Frey and on the

Thomas Gymnasium [Ewha Archives]

49th Anniversary of Ewha's founding, President Alice Appenzeller, Dean Helen Kim, faculty, staff, and 450 students celebrated with devotions at the chapel on the Chung Dong campus. There was excitement in the air as this was the day of the College's move to the Sinchon campus. In the chapel service, Alice Appenzeller gave a speech in which she said, "Our Ewha is the crystallization of prayers and love of many people of all walks of life from the world. There is no one person who built Ewha. Ewha was born from the love of many throughout the world."[14]

After the chapel devotion, President Appenzeller held a picture of the first Principal of Ewha, Mrs. Mary Scranton, and Dean Helen Kim held the photograph of her beloved teacher and founder of Ewha College, Miss Lulu Frey, as they and the faculty, staff and students marched to the new campus. The walk of two miles to the new Sinchon campus was exhilarating as were the hymns and prayers of thanksgiving expressed along the way. They arrived at Pfeiffer Hall, stood on its stone steps, and

Celebrating on steps of Pfeiffer Hall after arrival to new Sinchon campus, March 9, 1935
[Ewha Archives]

continued celebrating the opening of a new chapter of the remarkable history of Korean women, Ewha, and Korea. Pfeiffer Hall, now standing just as splendidly as it did on that day, is a majestic building made of granite brought from Songdo Island.

In the celebration opening the new campus, Bishop Herbert Welch, the first Resident Bishop in Korea of the Methodist Episcopal Church, United States of America, delivered a special dedication speech that expressed the profound meaning of the occasion. Among his comments, he reminded all those present that "Neither a beautiful site nor magnificent building will be the glory of the college, but the sound personalities which the school produces."[15]

The following year, Ewha celebrated its 50th Anniversary on May 31, 1936. The educational progress taking place on the Ewha Sinchon campus stood as a shining beacon of the miracle of Ewha. Ewha had

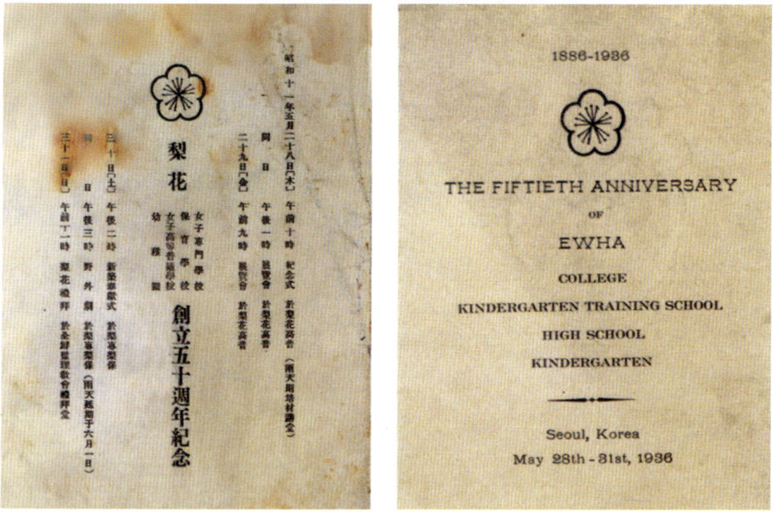
梨花
創立五十週年紀念
女子專門學校
保育學校
女子高等普通學校
幼稚園

1886-1936
THE FIFTIETH ANNIVERSARY
OF
EWHA
COLLEGE
KINDERGARTEN TRAINING SCHOOL
HIGH SCHOOL
KINDERGARTEN
Seoul, Korea
May 28th - 31st, 1936

50th Anniversary program, 1936 [Ewha Archives]

blossomed in spite of the hardships of the previous half-century, including social strife, Japanese domination, World War I, and a severe world economic depression. In her opening remarks at the celebration, President Appenzeller asserted, "I can feel your friendship towards Ewha and your trust in its future. We now wish to proceed with even greater faith and devotion towards the new age ahead of us."[16]

President Appenzeller stressed hope, faith, and prayers as being the strengths which had made Ewha possible. For those who loved Ewha, there was no distinction between the East and the West, or man or woman.[17]

A great many people, with unstinting love, sent generous gifts to Ewha. During the fifty years of Ewha history, a pivotal network of friends for Ewha from America, Korea, Canada, and Australia had been built through the connections of WFMS, Mission Boards, and churches. In celebration of the 50th Founding Anniversary, President Appenzeller conceptualized a script for a drama, *The River*. Professor Lee Hee-seung wrote the script and the students played the drama with dancing and mu-

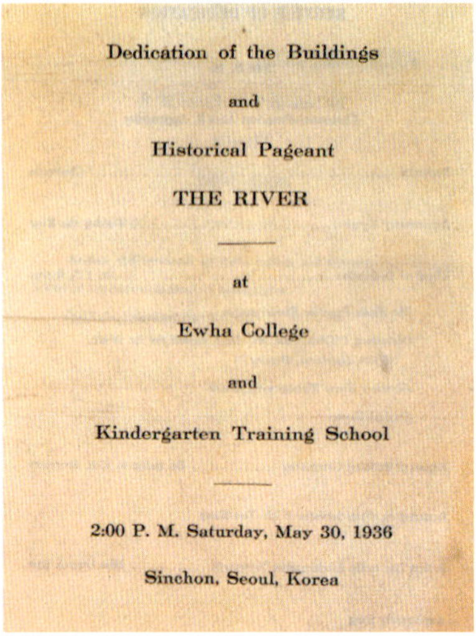

Dedication of the Buildings

and

Historical Pageant

THE RIVER

at

Ewha College

and

Kindergarten Training School

2:00 P. M. Saturday, May 30, 1936

Sinchon, Seoul, Korea

Ewha's 50th Anniversary program *The River* cover [Ewha Archives]

sic. The dance choreography was composed and directed by Professor Kim Shin-shil. The drama had five episodes depicting the history of 50 years of coming of age for Ewha College. The dance depicted a drop of water which became a stream, a river and then the ocean to symbolize the history of Ewha.[18]

President Appenzeller's concept for the 50th Anniversary drama seems an especially appropriate metaphor to describe

Ewha's 50th Anniversary *The River* drama, 1936 [Ewha Archives]

the spirit and impact of Ewha as a *River of Faith*. Starting modestly and ever growing because of the efforts of many, mostly women, working across national boundaries and generations, Ewha led the way for the education, liberation, and empowerment of Korean women. These enlightened women, in turn, joined the *River of Faith* in ever increasing numbers to change the status of females for the betterment of all society.

Part 2

Establishing Global Networks: 1936-1967

Ewha Cooperative Board in North America

Beginning in the 1930s, with Ewha President Appenzeller's leadership, actions were initiated to draw together, organize, and formalize ad hoc actions by organizations, individuals (missionaries, Koreans including alumnae and friends of Ewha), and churches to better coordinate and marshal support for Ewha. Sparsely documented, history does not definitively record the details of when, where, and how these efforts took place.

It is known that President Appenzeller advocated the creation of the Ewha Womans University Cooperating Board in North America, and historical documents mention that it was formed by her mission friends in Cincinnati, Ohio in 1933. Appenzeller asked those who had served as missionaries in Korea to form the Cooperating Board. The Ewha Womans University Press publication, *The 100 Years of Ewha Historical Documents and Artifacts*, indicated that President Appenzeller asked the Woman's Division of Christian Service of the Methodist Church to organize the "Ewha College Cooperating Committee" in order to support Ewha College. The Committee was organized in Cincinnati, Ohio, in 1938.[19] However, the Committee was not able to function because the Japanese colonial government imposed increasingly restrictive pressures that resulted in President Appenzeller's resignation in 1939. In late 1940, Appenzeller and other missionaries left Korea. This and World War II brought an extended hiatus to organizational efforts.

After the end of World War II, support for Ewha vigorously resumed. On November 23, 1946, the Ewha Womans University Cooperating Board in North America began operation with trustee members formally nominated by the Woman's Division of the Methodist Church and the Woman's Missionary Society of the United Church of Canada. The Cooperating Board members served three-year terms. Mrs. J. M. Avann was the Cooperating Board's first chair.[20]

Mr. Thomas Hobbs, Secretary for Korea for the British and Foreign Bible Society and Mrs. Edna Van Fleet Hobbs were appointed as Executive Secretaries for the Ewha Cooperating Board. The Canadian Mission Board joined the Ewha Board. The Ewha Cooperating Board in North America was incorporated in the State of New York. It became the coordinating body for providing essential financial support for Ewha.

The Cooperating Board assumed the role the WFMS had played, continuing a legacy of educational mission that had begun with Mrs. Mary Scranton's arrival in Korea in 1885.

An Evolving Partnership: 1930s

The 1930s saw different attempts to create cooperating committees or boards for the purpose of providing support for Ewha Womans College. Included was an organization composed of Supporting Trustees initiated in 1934 by mostly Koreans in Korea. President Appenzeller and members of WFMS in the U.S. formed the Ewha Womans University Cooperating Board in 1938. The actual date of formation is not definite, as it was writ-

Trustee Supporters Association [Ewha Archives]

ten in an essay by Ewha alumna Dr. Kilchai Yim that the Ewha Cooperating Board was formed in 1933 by the request of President Appenzeller. Dr. Yim mentioned that she heard that the Ewha Cooperating Board was formed during the year she graduated from Ewha, which was 1933.[21]

Ewha College established a Supporters Association for Ewha College which held its initial meeting in February 1933 in the auditorium of Ewha College in Chung Dong, Seoul. Twenty-five council Members were elected.[22]

In 1938, Ewha faced another challenging chapter for supporting and managing Ewha. The Japanese colonial government marked Ewha as the product of American missionaries, resulting in President Appenzeller resignation. She nominated Dr. Helen Kim to succeed her as President.

Dr. Appenzeller quoted Shakespeare to Dr. Helen Kim at the time, "Some are born great, some achieve greatness, and some have greatness thrust upon them." She added, "You are in the third category. You will have to take the presidency whether you like it or not."[23]

Ewha campus, 1938 [Ewha Archives]

The responsibility to carry on Ewha College then fell on Dr. Helen Kim's shoulders. Included among many serious challenges being faced was one of immediate financial calamity. The Japanese government stopped allowing any financial support from sources external to Korea, thereby cutting off vital funding. WFMS and other mission organizations had routinely supported about two-thirds of the Ewha budget.[24]

Leaders from all walks of Korean society joined to assist Ewha as higher education for women was one of the keys for the long-sought Korean independence. In 1933, a support committee had been formed by Koreans and chaired by a well-known Korean businessman. Although suppressed by the Japanese, it appears the support committee functioned in the years that followed. With the departure of missionaries and loss of external support, the newly appointed President Helen Kim no doubt called on the support committee members to help mitigate the impacts of the loss of financial assistance from mission sources. Two major donors came forward to help at this time of great distress. Chu Tae-kyoung, a widow, donated her entire life's savings, equivalent to $25,000, and Sohn Chang-sik, a Korean businessman living in China, provided a sum of $125,000.[25]

In 1943, Ewha successfully established a Board of Trustees under the leadership of President Helen Kim. Among the list of Trustees were some Americans named in absentia, including Dr. Appenzeller.

Ewha Transitions and Grows: Post World War II

From 1939 through World War II, Ewha's indigenous leadership courageously managed and funded Ewha sufficiently for survival during extremely difficult times. Also in 1939, the Methodist organization in the U.S. underwent change. The Methodist Church was created from a merger of the Methodist Protestant Church, the Methodist Episcopal Church South, and the Methodist Episcopal Church. With the merger, the powerful woman's missionary agency, the WFMS, lost its independency. In order to retain autonomy of women's work in the church, the women's group succeeded in establishing the Woman's Division of Christian Service. The new entity had the right to control funds, appoint missionaries, and organize mission work for women and children.

Following the end of World War II, the extremely helpful exchange of East and West at Ewha through mission and other avenues was restored through the newly created Ewha Womans University Cooperating Board in North America. In early February 1946, President Helen Kim made her first return trip to the United States in 15 years to attend the National Convention of the YWCA. Shortly thereafter, President Kim attended a meeting of the evolving Ewha Cooperating Board on March 21, 1946 in New York. In the fall of 1946, the evacuated missionary teachers began to return. Dr. Alice Appenzeller was the first to return to Korea. Then, seven others came. Only those that had passed the age limit for retirement did not return. Dr. Appenzeller and the others took on full schedules for teaching subjects they had formerly taught.

Cover of Dr. Helen Kim's memoir [Chang Hyun Shin Geer]

The year 1946 was an exciting year for Ewha College. A new era opened for women in Korea as Ewha was granted approval to be a four-year institution by the Ministry of Education on August 15, 1946. Ewha Womans University was inaugurated and structured to have three separate colleges, Medicine, Art, and Academics. Ewha was positioned to address the surge of young women in Korea aspiring for further education.

In September 1948, Dr. Helen Kim presented to the Ewha Cooperating Board the University's request for approval of the construction of a science building at an estimated cost of $140,000. The Board approved US$161,000 for the science building and other facilities. The fund was managed and disbursed by the recommendation of the Woman's Division of Christian Service of the Methodist Church. The funds came from the Cooperating Board, of which, $70,000 was received from the Pfeiffer estates.

On February 20, 1950, Dr. Appenzeller was leading the chapel service in the University Chapel. As she was reading *Matthew 7:15, Beware of False Prophets*, her voice faltered and became indistinct. While being carried to the ambulance, Dr. Helen Kim held her hand. She passed away shortly thereafter at nearby Severance Hospital.

Dr. Helen Kim, in her memoir, *Grace Sufficient*, describes her final moment with Dr. Appenzeller,

> *... she moved her right hand as if trying to grasp something. I took hold of her hand and she held mine tightly until we were ready to close the ambulance door. She was not able to speak, but I knew this last handclasp meant exactly the same thing she had said as she held my hand*

Appenzeller Science Building [Ewha Archives]

when she had to evacuate in 1940. "I am sorry to go, but glad to leave everything in your hands. I will pray for you and God will help you."[26]

Among her many accomplishments to the benefit of Ewha, Dr. Appenzeller demonstrated successful fundraising during her long tenure at Ewha, particularly when she was its President. So it was fitting that after her passing, her many beloved friends established the Alice Appenzeller Scholarship Endowment for an exchange scholar program. Prof. Chung Ii-sook, one of the recipients, studied Religious Education at Northwestern University, and later became Ewha's ninth president.

The science building was named Appenzeller Science Hall in 1958 in honor of Dr. Alice Appenzeller. Its architectural style is similar to Pfeiffer Hall.

The Ewha Cooperating Board in North America was proactive in seeking and providing support for the financial needs of Ewha. It was managed by both the Methodist Women's Division staff and Christian volunteers. The officers of the Board were Miss Henrietta Gibson (later Mrs.W. Earl Ledden), President, Mrs. Hugh D. Taylor, Vice President, Mrs. J. Wesley Masland, Treasurer, and Mrs. Frank E. Baker, Recording Secretary.

The official minutes of the Ewha Cooperating Board were first recorded at a meeting on September 15, 1948 at a meeting in New York, with Mrs. Velma Maynor as chair pro-tem. The Cooperating Board fulfilled the legal requirements to operate under the auspices of the Methodist Division of Christian Service.

The organizational relationships among the Ewha Cooperating Board of North America, the Board of Ewha Trustees in Seoul, and the Ewha President were tightly delineated, so that even President Helen Kim's travel in the U.S. and the expenses covering her travel required approval by the Board of Directors of the Ewha Cooperating Board.[27]

The operational procedures of the Cooperating Board were cumbersome as evident from Board minutes:

> *Requests coming from Ewha Womans University in Korea are sent to Mr. and Mrs. Thomas Hobbs, Executive secretaries, who in turn present such requests to the Ewha Cooperating Board of North America. Such matters as should have action or approval of the Woman's Division of Christian Service should be submitted to the Foreign Department, through the Executive Secretary for Korea of the Woman's Division. The Executive Committee of Ewha Womans University should be asked to send a copy of all such requests having to do with the Methodist Boards, to the Central Council in Korea.*[28]

Additionally, the United Church of Canada shared a partnership with Ewha Cooperating Board in North America through appropriations of scholarships for Ewha students studying in Canada.

Sustaining the Challenges: 1951-1961

Starting on June 25, 1950, the tragic Korean War engulfed all of South Korea as the armed forces of North Korea attacked across the 38th parallel. From late 1950 to 1953 Ewha became a university in exile in Busan. Fortunately, financial support for Ewha flowed continuously from the World Division of the General Board of Global Ministries of The Methodist Church which recognized the urgency of supporting Christian higher education in Korea.

Miss Margaret Billingsley was the Executive Secretary for Korea and a staff member of the Woman's Division of Christian Service of Methodist Church. She played a critical role in the delivery of financial assistance to meet needs of Ewha Womans University while accommodating procedures required by the World Division of the United Methodist Church.

The Ewha Womans University Cooperating Board in North America

Ewha's evacuee campus in Busan during the Korean War [Ewha Archives]

Miss Margaret Billingsley at Ewha's 1949 May Day Celebration [Dr. Hai Won Chang Archives]

was incorporated on May 3, 1951 pursuant to the Membership Corporation Law of the State of New York. Henrietta Gibson (later Henrietta Gibson Ledden), Elizabeth Masland, Bessie Kim, Margaret Billingsley, Margaret Forsyth, and Ruth Taylor constituted a committee to act as incorporators of the corporation, with power to do any and all things necessary to conduct the corporation.

Under the new organizational structure, the Pfeiffer Endowment assets that had been held by the WFMS were transferred to the Woman's Division of Christian Service for the disbursement for maintaining the Pfeiffer Administration building.

The post-Korean War years brought even more challenges for the Ewha Cooperating Board in North America's support of Ewha University. Among the challenges included meeting the needs of the increased student enrollments, the rehabilitation of war-damaged buildings, and the construction of new buildings. One of critical assistances carried out by the Cooperating Board was the ecumenical effort to face the crisis of increased student enrollment through the provision of scholarships for students, particularly those that had escaped from North Korea. Miss Billingsley visited the Ewha University Evacuee Campus in Busan in 1951 and reported to the Cooperating Board of the imperative for scholarship funds.

The United Church of Canada and the Presbyterian Board were asked to participate in providing scholarships for Ewha. The United Church of Canada contributed scholarship funds for students. Also, the U.S. Presbyterian Church supported a faculty member to teach at Ewha.

Building construction was addressed via a major building proposal advanced by Ewha. In June 1956,

... the Ewha University Board of Trustees asked the Ewha Cooperating Board in North America to assume half the cost of the proposed $1,500,000 building program. After the suggestions made by Mr. Too Pyung Park and Mr. Tong Keun Lee, members of the Ewha University Board of Trustees, the proposal of the building budget was moved to have the Chairs, Miss Gibson and Mrs. Masland, carry it to the Cooperating Board in the North America the decision of the Ewha University Board of Managers to assume half the cost of the estimated $1,500,000 construction program if the Cooperating Board would assume the other half. This program of construction would cover the following buildings; library, dormitory, hospital, new central heating system, completion of student hall building, a heating system of student building, dining hall, a museum, and plastering and fire escape for the Grand Auditorium, as well as a heating system of the auditorium ...[29]

Through the Woman's Division of Christian Service, Board of Missions of the Methodist Church, Board of World Mission, and the United Church of Canada, $722,961 of the amount requested by the Ewha Trustees in 1956 was sent to Ewha by 1962.

"The Best is Yet to Be": 1961 and Beyond

The decade of the 1960's largely corresponded to the planning and initial "take-off" phase of the Korean national economy which led to the ensuing decades of high growth and rapid industrialization. The Korean government focused on the essential role of education to meet the human resource needs of the country, especially to meet the requirements for industrialization. The Ministry of Education implemented strong regulations concerning the establishment and expansion of private universities.[30]

Ewha faced another wave of change as Korea underwent political, economic, and social changes resulting from the May 16, 1961 military

The Welch-Ryang Auditorium [Ewha Archives]

coup d'état that placed General Park Chung Hee into the national presidency. President Park vigorously pursued a policy of export-oriented industrialization. As part of that policy, a University Restructuring Law was implemented that established quotas drastically reducing student enrollments and closing certain university departments, thereby precipitating the discharge of faculty and staff because of financial difficulties brought on by lost tuition. Universities lost their rights to confer degrees, replaced by nationwide testing conducted by the government that determined qualification for degrees. Additionally, the government dictated that faculty of age sixty or more be retired. President Helen Kim was among those forced to relinquish their positions because of age.

On September 30, 1961, Dr. Okgill Kim was inaugurated as President of Ewha. Dr. Helen Kim, in her farewell address at the ceremony, encouraged the faculty and staff to look forward with hope by quoting Robert Browning from his poem, *Rabbi Ben Ezra*,

Grow old along with me!
The best is yet to be,
The last of life, for which the first was made:
Our times are in His hand
Who saith, 'A whole I planned,
Youth shows but half; trust God: see all, nor be afraid!'

After stepping down from the presidency, Dr. Helen Kim became the Chair of the Ewha University Board of Trustees and focused on financial development for the progress of Ewha University.

The combined energies of Dr. Helen Kim as the Chair of the Ewha Board of Trustees and Dr. Okgill Kim as the new President Ewha University, tenaciously led Ewha through a period of continual progress. Dr. Helen Kim invited Dr. Burnice H. Jarman to evaluate Ewha Womans University in terms of status and potential as a viable institution of higher education from a global perspective. He was asked to help set up a two-year self-study of the University. Dr. Jarman, from George Washington University, was Chief Advisor of Higher Education of the United States Operation Mission, Seoul, Korea.

The results of the study reported strengths and weaknesses. It described Ewha as a well-run university with an indomitable spirit to carry out its goals. The weaknesses and needs focused on the level of the faculty's academic training, as few professors had graduate degrees.

It was recommended that faculty members receive more professional training and there be more contact time between faculty and students. To mitigate these weaknesses, steps had to be taken to increase the number of faculty members and to provide opportunities for more faculty members to receive advanced training. The strengthening of Ewha's graduate schools was recommended.

Dr. Jarman described the University in glowing and superlative terms:

Ewha Womans University plays a national role in women's higher education unmatched by any other institution in the free world. Ewha enrolls one half of the Korean girls who attend college. If Korea is to achieve political economic independence in a democratic frame work, she must give her daughters opportunity for higher education equal to that provided for her sons. In a man-centered culture Ewha Womans University is Korea's brightest hope for a better tomorrow. Let us all resolve to make this possibility a reality.[31]

Within the fast growing industrializing society during the 1960s, Ewha University vigorously pursued progress. The Ewha Cooperating Board partnered with the World Division and the Woman's Division of the Methodist Church and the United Church of Canada and the Ewha Supporting Committee in Seoul to facilitate the progress.

Shaping Ewha's Future as a Global University: 1966 and Onward

At its Annual Founder's Day ceremony on May 31, 1966, Ewha celebrated its 80 years of progress towards educating women in Korea. At the celebration, Trustee Chair Helen Kim and President Okgill Kim spoke of looking forward and deliberating on a vision for Ewha for the next 80 years and beyond. The vision was to grow the University and provide opportunities for all women to be intellectualized so that women could contribute towards modernizing Korea.

Dr. Helen Kim spoke,

... In the perspective of higher civilized society we need to incorporate our traditional culture and the model of the advanced culture of the West in order to create an ideal civilization ... We need to educate our students to meet these needs to prepare for the next eighty years and an-

Mrs. W. Earl Ledden and Charles Gibson Hall [International Foundation Archives]

other eighty years. We will educate students to seek the truth, the goodness, and the beauty. We need to develop science programs to educate students in order to meet the human resource needs of a modern industrialized nation. We need to develop programs in the social sciences so our graduates could serve the various communities through social services and rural community reform.

President Okgill Kim eloquently noted,

"For the hand that rocks the cradle is the hand that rules the world." [William Ross Wallace] *Likewise we have a noble mission that in faith we see the truth and in hope we advance it diligently. "Then you will know the truth, and the truth will set you free."* [*Gospel John 8:32*] *The purpose of learning is to be engaged in what we learn about the truth and contribute our learning to Koreans and mankind. ... We will endeavor for study in many areas and serve community, society and family with what we have learned ... .*[32]

Included in the Ewha 80th Anniversary Celebration was the recognition of three donors. Mrs. W. Henrietta Ledden was a former member of the Ewha Cooperating Board who made great contributions to the growing University both spiritually and materially. In gratitude for her devoted service for Ewha and in honor of her father, Mr. Charles Gibson, who made her gift possible, the additional gymnasium was dedicated as Charles Gibson Hall. A McCreless Room was dedicated to Mr. and Mrs. S. E. McCreless, and a Masland Room was dedicated to Mrs. J. Wesley Masland for her dedication and her spiritual and material contribution.

By 1967, $1,009,566 had been sent to Ewha University over an 11-year period as the fulfillment of the agreement made in 1956 to raise $1,000,000 for a building fund. Included in the raised funding was $25,000 from the Kresge Foundation.

Part 3

A New Era, "The Sweet Fragrance of Knowledge"

Ewha Decade Development Committee: 1966–1971

During the 1960s, Ewha University moved forward with a newly defined vision to become a world-class institution of higher learning. The enrollment of students exceeded 8,000 and the number of faculty members went over 300. The university grew its academic programs to nine colleges and 40 departments, and expanded the Graduate School. The ultimate goal was "to make Ewha a mecca of learning for the women leaders of the world." Work towards achieving this goal was led by Dr. Helen Kim, President of the Board of Trustees, and Dr. Okgill Kim, the President of the University.

The momentum of the first 80 years of accomplishments through the concerted efforts of many across generations and national boundaries had set the stage for the new goal of advancing Ewha to premier university status. To realize the goal, the leaders of Ewha University decided to seek funds for $20,000,000. The purpose of the proposed funding was to support initiatives including scholarly research, professional exchange, emphasis on science and technology, creation of law and business administration colleges, construction of a new hospital and a science building with various lab facilities, expansion of the graduate school program, strengthening the professionalism of the faculty, and the establishment of a Research Institute of Women Studies.

The United States in the 1960s was undergoing its own turmoil associated with social and political change. The conservatism and social conformity of the 1950s was being questioned and forced to give way. The civil rights movement dominated in the first half of the 1960s. During the *March on Washington for Jobs and Freedom* rally in August 1963, Martin Luther King made his never-to-be forgotten "*I Have a Dream*" speech. Soon afterward, President Lyndon B. Johnson signed the Civil Rights Act of 1964.

A new wave of feminism in the United States and around the world gained its own momentum during the early 1960s. The conflict in Vietnam War escalated, as did civil unrest from the anti-war movement. Primarily due to the Vietnam War, the image of Asia in the U.S. was negatively impacted.

For almost a century of women's mission, the focus in the U.S. was to send missionaries and funds to help change the lives of women and girls in foreign lands such as Korea. By the 1960s, new challenges and issues had emerged. In 1964, The Methodist Church experienced a restructuring, and in 1968 full clergy rights for women were affirmed. Collectively, the economic, political, and social changes impacted the conditions of support for women's education in Asia.

At the Ewha Cooperating Board annual meeting held in New York on May 1, 1967, Dr. Helen Kim presented the Ewha University Decade Development Program proposal of $20,000,000. She asked the Cooperating Board to raise $10,000,000, with another $10,000,000 to be raised in Korea. The Cooperating Board was in sympathy with the projects, but some members felt the Board was unable to consider undertaking the sponsorship of the new Development Program campaign funds because of its organizational structure bound with the Methodist Church. However, the Board decided that funds raised from other sources could be deposited into the Cooperating Board as its purpose was to receive gifts from all sources for Ewha Womans University and that funds for the development program could be received by the Board.

It was also agreed that administration of the funds would be handled by the Board. While the Cooperating Board played an oversight role in managing all the funds for Ewha, a new fundraising organization would be created in lieu of "Ewha Womans University Development Committee." Those at the meeting included were Dr. Harry Denman, Mrs. W. Earl Hillman, Miss Margaret Forsyth, Mrs. Bessie Kim, Mrs. Earl Ledden, Mr. Leonard Peale, Dr. Allen B. Rice, Bishop Hazen G. Werner, Dr. Kilchai K. Yim, Dr. Sam Smith, and Mrs. Wayne Lamb. These attending members and Miss Margret Billingsley, who was the Executive Director for Ewha Cooperating Board in liaison of the Woman's Division of the Methodist Church, became members. Dr. Henry P. Van Dusen and Mrs. Henrietta G. Ledden became Honorary Chairpersons. The purpose of this committee was to promote the campaign, but not to handle the funds.[33]

Ewha President Okgill Kim was the Vice Chair for the Decade Development Committee in Korea. The Central Office of the Decade Development Programwas located on the Ewha campus with branches in Washington, DC and New York City. Dr. Helen Kim appointed twelve members for the Development Program in the U.S. The key members were Dr. Hai Won Chang and her husband Dr. Soon Man Rhim, Dr. Chang Woon Huh Choo and her husband Dr. Yung Bin Choo, Dr. Bumsun Lee, Mrs/Dr. Hyang Won Lee, and Dr. Kilchai K. Yim. The Charter members of the Washington, DC branch were Dr. and Mrs. C. C. Choi, Mr. Sae Sun Kim, Dr. Myung Soon Lim, and Dr. Henry Oh. Those U.S. key members and charter members were graduates or members of families of Ewha graduates.

Ewha Womans University Development Committee: 1967–1969

In 1967, Dr. Helen Kim reorganized the development program and named it the Ewha Womans University Development Committee. She asked Dr. Harry Denman, a Methodist evangelist and friend, to be Chair of the Committee. Mr. Dong Jo Kim, Korean Ambassador to the U.S. was a member, and Dr. Henry P. Van Dusen and Mrs. Henrietta Gibson Ledden were appointed as Honorary Chairs. Honorary Sponsors included fourteen Bishops of the Methodist Church and dozens of friends of Ewha. The Honorary membership of 85 persons included Mrs. Laurence Rockerfeller, Bishop James C. Baker, Pearl Buck, Justice and Mrs. Thurgood Marshall, Dr. C.W. Mayo, Dr. Dorothy McConnell, Bishop W. Earl Ledden, Ambassador and Mrs. Yong Shik Kim, and Mrs. Clare Booth Luce.

Mr. Moon Pyo Hong, an English major graduate of Seoul National University, was hired to assist Dr. Helen Kim while she was working on

1969 Ewha Development Board Meeting with Dr. Helen Kim [International Foundation Archives]

the Ewha University Development project. Mr. Hong drove his own car to transport Dr. Kim when she traveled from city to city to meet Ewha alumnae and promote the creation of local Ewha Alumnae Chapters. Road journeys were made to Lake Junaluska (North Carolina), Boston, South Bend (Indiana), Chicago, Detroit, Toronto, Hartford and New Haven (Connecticut), and Alexandria (Virginia) as she worked tirelessly to earn friends for the Ewha Development Program. While travelling, Dr. Kim stayed in YMCA hotels with low rates or in the homes of Ewha alumnae in order to minimize the expenses.

The Ewha Development Program hired Mrs. Alice Pennington as Executive Director and paid for her apartment in Silver Spring, a Maryland suburb of Washington, DC, to be used as the program office. She worked closely with Dr. Helen Kim and also with Dr. H. Denman and Mrs. Hillman to seek funds for the Development program. She sent out 25,000 pieces of mail to promote the Development Program and the Ewha Cooperating Board in North America. She sent all incoming funds to the Cooperating Board and gifts of stocks were made out for the Development Fund to be sent to the Irving Trust Company where Cooperating Board funds were managed. Funds that were raised were managed by the Ewha Cooperating Board.

Development Program brochure
[International Foundation Archives]

Dr. Helen Kim started local Ewha Alumnae Chapters to raise money for the Development Program in Hawaii (goal, $200,000), Los Angeles (goal, $100,000), Washington, DC, Maryland and Virginia (goal, $300,000). In her report, the Committee stated the goal of recruiting 100,000 sponsors giving a minimum of $100 each to raise a minimum of $10,000,000.

In February 1967, Dr. Helen Kim traveled to Honolulu, Los Angeles, Washington, DC, Hartford, New Haven, Boston, and New York to recruit friends and Ewha graduates for participation in the Development Program. Her fundraising travel expenses were covered by the Development Committee. The graduates and the family of the graduates centered on raising the funds for Ewha University Development Program.

The mailing list of potential donors was near 5,000, including Ewha graduates. Many video programs and booklets about Ewha were distributed. A brochure, embellished with a pear flower and the statement "The sweet fragrance of knowledge," was produced and distributed, with a strong call for support, "Please give! Ewha needs your help! $10,000,000 is our goal!"

During 1968, in spite of the dedicated fundraising, the Development Program was not progressing as well as anticipated and the funds raised were less than the costs of the Executive Director's salary and office. Consequently, Mrs. Pennington was released and the Silver Spring Development Program office was closed.

The Methodist Board of Missions had just completed its restructuring, many of its members retired, and the entire make up of the Board of Missions was changed. The socio-political climate of the U.S. was in flux as it faced the American counter-culture revolution including the civil rights movement, the anti-Vietnam War movement, and the rise of feminism. Mrs. Margaret Billingsley, the Executive Director for Ewha Cooperating Board in North America as a representative of the Woman Division of Global Mission of the United Methodist Church, retired. She had played a critical role for assisting Ewha. Ms. Peggy Billings, an Assistant for Mrs. Billingsley, became the Executive Director of the Woman Division for Ewha University. [In April 1968, The Methodist Church united with the Evangelical United Brethern Church to form The United Methodist Church.]

On January 17, 1969, the World Division of the Board of Missions issued a revised delineation of its relationship with the Ewha Cooperating Board in North America. It was necessitated by the fact that the Board of Missions was associated with approximately 1000 institutions in 50 countries while operating with limited human and financial resources. The new working relationship would embodied the following:

1. The Cooperating Board will have its own autonomy in determining its membership and in drawing from other spheres of educational and economic resources.
2. The World Division of the Board of Missions will relate to the Cooperating Board through representatives, but the Cooperating Board would in no sense be a committee of the World Division.
3. The Cooperating Board will have its own determination of its responsibilities in relation to Ewha University.
4. The World Division of the Board of Missions continues to have objectives and concerns in relation to Ewha University, and will seek to make these objectives and concerns known through its representatives on the Cooperating Board.

The newly stated relationship between the World Division of the Board of Missions and Ewha Womans University paved the way allowing friends of Ewha to have greater autonomy in fundraising and recruiting sponsors and sponsoring organizations. The stage was now set for fundraising more in alignment with needs as determined by Ewha and more directly delivered to Ewha.

Fundraising began to bear fruit. As of March 31, 1969, total gifts received were $179,574, of which $142,298 was transferred to Ewha University, and $37,276 was held reserved in a special account for a nurses' dormitory at Ewha.

On May 31, 1969, Dr. Hyo Sub Sohn, President of Ewha Womans

University Alumnae Association, Boston Chapter, held a fundraising event for the Development Program. Each Ewha alumna in the Boston area was asked to sponsor with a $100 donation.

New York Alumnae held a highly successful "Benefit Ball for Ewha Womans University Development" on September 20, 1969 at the Park Sheraton Hotel.

The Emerging International Foundation for Ewha Womans University: 1969-1970

In June 1969, one of the projects to promote Ewha University in the U.S. was the establishment of an Ewha Room at Lambuth Inn, Lake Junaluska, North Carolina, which also served to welcome a visit by Dr. Helen Kim. The Lambuth Inn is a retreat and conference center of Christian hospitality, a place of spiritual enrichment, and leader development to meet the needs of The United Methodist Church. The Ewha Room was opened on July 4th, 1969 in order to introduce Ewha and the Ewha Development Program. The Ewha Room was arranged by Dr. and Mrs. J. Manning Potts. It was decorated with many beautiful Korean objects which Dr. Helen Kim

Dr. Helen Kim's visit to the Ewha Room in Lambuth Inn, Lake Juanuska [International Foundation Archives]

and Ewha alumnae provided. Dr. Helen Kim stayed at Lambuth Inn for three weeks. The Ewha Room was visited by 500 people and was well received. The Ewha Room subsequently became the Korea Room.

During her stay at the Lambuth Inn, Dr. Helen Kim met privately with Dr. Harry Denman, Chair of the Ewha Development Committee. It is presumed they had discussions relating to future development plans in view of the lackluster performance of the Development Committee approach. One outcome of their meeting was Dr. Denman's resignation as chair of the Committee, setting the stage for change in organizational structure.

Soon after the Lake Junaluska trip, Dr. Kim and Mr. Moon Pyo Hong traveled to Washington, DC. There, they stayed at the home of Dr. and Mrs. C. C. Choi in Alexandria, Virginia. Mrs. Choi was an Ewha graduate. While there, Dr. Helen Kim consulted with Mr. Keh Soo Park, an attorney in Arlington, Virginia. Mr. Park assisted in registering the International Foundation for Ewha Womans University as a non-profit organization incorporated in the District of Columbia. A year later, in June 1969, the Foundation was moved to New York and was located in a small space in the office of a Korean businessman at 45th street and Madison Avenue. Two months later, the office was moved to the Interchurch Center, Riverside Drive, New York, through the help of Dr. Van Dusen, then Vice President of the Interchurch Center.

"Win a Friend for Ewha." ... "Right Here and Now."

In October 1969, after working for eight months setting up the future Ewha Foundation, Dr. Helen Kim headed for Seoul, Korea. Mr. Moon Pyo Hong drove her to the Kennedy Airport to see her off. He recalled that she was quietly crying. "I have never seen her cry so much. She kept saying, 'How can I pay back all the debts I owe to all my friends?' She went into the airplane with tears." Is it possible she knew that this was the end of her last journey to her second home? [Personal interview]

Dr. Helen Kim, 1899-1970
[Ewha Archives]

During the latter part of her stay in the U.S., dissent swept Korean college campuses because of the proposed constitutional amendment referendum allowing President Park Chung Hee to serve a third term. She was pleased Ewha students expressed their opinions without forcing the closing of the University. Voters approved the tenure amendment in October 1969. Regardless of the challenges of fundraising and the political unrest in both the U.S. and Korea, Dr. Kim's passion for Ewha's progress could not be deterred. However, her eight months of traveling in the U.S. had taken a toll on her fragile health. Regardless, her spirit of "the best yet to be" kept her river of faith flowing.

Dr. Helen Kim asked Mr. Hong to send out a letter she had prepared before leaving the U.S. of greetings and promotion of Ewha University to the friends of Ewha. The letter, sent on November 10, 1969, included the following excerpts:

Dear Friends,

To many of you I really owe a letter and I would like so much writing a personal one instead of this general report. Please read it in that spirit and overlook its generalization.

As our promotional material to use in all these contacts we have a thirty minute documentary, sound movie film called 'Life at Ewha.' We have just published a new brochure enough for all of you to have plenty copies ... Please use them.

There are more places to go and more friends to win for Ewha all over the world. Let us proceed from our own homes, towns, clubs and groups "right here and now." Let the words, "Win a Friend for Ewha" be our motto for 1970.

On February 10, 1970, Dr. Helen K. Kim passed away in Seoul. Faith, internationalism, self-reliance, and empowerment of women through education had been ingrained in her life's mission. Just as those who came before her, she had picked up where the previous generation left off, made her contribution, and then passed it on to others. Like her predecessors, Dr. Helen Kim exhibited the same supreme confidence in Ewha's future.

Mrs. Estelle Hillman, President of Ewha Cooperating Board in North America, 1969
[International Foundation Archives]

Mrs. Estelle Hillman, President, called to order the final annual meeting of the Ewha Cooperating Board in North America on April 14, 1970 at the New Yorker Hotel, New York. Ewha President Okgill Kim gave the report of Ewha's progress. Mrs. Hillman outlined the new relationships with the International Foundation for Ewha Womans University and stated the hope that all the committees would become one body under the Foundation. The Cooperating Board unanimously voted (1) to merge with the International Foundation as of April 1, 1970, and (2) to direct all funds designated to the Cooperating Board be received and processed by the International Foundation. It should be noted that Mrs. Hillman worked vigilantly to help Ewha for many years. She helped to promote the acquisition of funds through the Development Committee while chairing the Coordinating Board. She was a dear friend of Dr. Helen Kim.[34]

At the same meeting, the Ewha Development Committee, which had been under the leadership of Ms. Peggy Billings, gave unanimous consensus to merge with the International Foundation if it became a reality and if its members received invitations to become the members of the International Foundation.

Part 4

The International Foundation for Ewha Womans University

The Inaugural Meeting of the International Foundation: 1970

The Inaugural Meeting of the International Foundation for Ewha Womans University, Inc. was held on April 15, 1970 at the New Yorker Hotel, New York. Dr. James Laney, a friend of Dr. Helen Kim who later became the President of Emory University and subsequently served as the U.S. Ambassador to the Republic of Korea (1993-1996), opened the momentous meeting with a prayer.

Ms. Peggy Billings, Coordinator of the Mission Division of the United Methodist Church, served the roles of chair and moderator for the merger of the two parent organizations. The International Foundation became a reality through the unanimous consensus that the Ewha Cooperating Board and the Development Committee merge with the International Foundation for Ewha Womans University.

Ms. Billings, serving as Chair of the inaugural meeting, declared,

Recognizing the action of the Ewha Womans University Cooperating Board of North America, Inc., April 14, 1970, and the September 18, 1969, and April 14, 1970 actions of the Development Committee, we declare the inauguration of the new supporting body for Ewha Womans University in North America to be the International Foundation for Ewha Womans University, Inc.[35]

With this declaration, The International Foundation for Ewha Womans University, Inc., was born in the form as it exists today.

The names of charter members of the Foundation Board of Directors are listed in Appendix B. Twenty-eight members and three staff members were present at the meeting. President Okgill Kim represented Ewha. Several Ewha faculty members, including Prof. Kim Jung-ok, niece of Dr. Helen Kim, also participated.

Chair Billings appointed a committee to revise the Constitution, as follows.

Mrs. E. L. Hillman	Mrs. Maude Jensen
Mrs. F. K. Faist	Rev. Henry Oh
Dr. Charles Germany	Mr. P. William Lee
Mrs. Hilda Lee Dail	

Chair Billings also appointed a Nomination Committee for exploring possibilities for getting new members for the Foundation Board, including suggestions from members as to a President of the Foundation and other officers as needed.

Dr. Samuel Smith	Mr. Sae Sun Kim
Dr. James Laney (Elected Chair)	Mrs. Margaret Forsyth
Mrs. Bessie Kim	Mrs. Charles Tillett

Mrs. W. Earl Ledden | Dr. Okgill Kim (Advisor)
Mrs. J. A. Barclay

Mrs. Earl L. Hillman, who had been President of Ewha Cooperating Board in North America in 1969, made a summary statement regarding Ewha's relationship to the United States and Canada:

> *The history of Ewha's relationship to the United States and Canada is a close and continuous one from the founding of Ewha as a girl's school by an American missionary until today when we come to the inaugural meeting of the International Foundation for Ewha Womans University, Inc.*
>
> *There has been a steady flow, missionaries and teachers from the United States and Canada into Ewha, and a steady flow of Ewha teachers and students into Canada and the United States has enriched the cultural and economic life of the U.S. and Canada.*
>
> *Seldom has any person made such an impact on Methodist women in the United States as Dr. Helen Kim made. The International Foundation is her brain-child and we enter into this new relationship with joy and gratitude, and with great expectations for its future.*[36]

The new International Foundation began working immediately by conducting a brainstorming session. An Advisory Committee was formed in order to lay a solid cornerstone as the supporting body for Ewha University based on ideals of internationalism and ecumenical partnership, which Dr. Alice Appenzeller, Dr. Helen Kim, and others had exalted. The creation of the International Foundation upheld the dream of Helen Kim as the Foundation had embodied international and independent attributes in a self-reliant organization inviting friends for Ewha from all over the world. It was a realization of gratitude that Alice Appenzeller proclaimed on the day of the 50th Anniversary of its founding, "Ewha is the crystallization of prayers of all walks of life from all over the world." During the inaugural and subsequent meetings, responsibilities of the International Foundation Board members and procedural aspects regarding financial transitions were examined through sessions led by Ms. Billings.

Dr. Helen Kim had obviously identified Ms. Peggy Billings as a strong and helpful ally in helping to fulfill her dream of establishing and organizing the International Foundation for Ewha Womans University. Ms. Billings had served as a Methodist missionary in the Far East from 1952 to 1963, most of it in Korea, first in Pusan and later at the Tae Wha Social Service Center in Seoul. After her return to the United States in 1963, she went to work for the United Methodist Church, devoting her life to racial justice, civil rights, community action, peace, international affairs, and women's issues. She was Deputy General Secretary of the World Division of the General Board of Global Ministries of the United Methodist Church in the 1970s.

Ms. Billings earned a B.S. degree from Millsaps College in 1950 and received an M.A. degree from Teachers College, Columbia University in 1958. In 1986, she was awarded an honorary doctorate by Ewha Womans University at its Centennial Celebration. She was a visiting Professor of Church and Society at the School of Theology, Emory University in Atlanta, Georgia.

For the 40th Anniversary Booklet of the International Foundation, she wrote of the time when the International Foundation was being conceptualized,

> *In 1968, Dr. Helen Kim invited Margaret Billingsley, staff of Women's Division for Korea, Henrietta Gibson, the Treasurer of the women's Division and me at the Warwick Hotel, not sure why we were being summoned. But when Helen Kim called, you went! ... she shared her dream for an International Foundation for Ewha ... Great divisions in the (American) society over Vietnam war and the Civil Rights struggle*

had surfaced, having a profound impact on the churches, too. There were many changes in personnel and structures in the churches. It was a very different scene. It was certainly not an easy time to talk about creating a new international organization to raise funds for a university in another country. ... How could we say 'no'? We pointed out the problems, but naturally, we agreed to do what she asked of us.[37]

The International Foundation founding members in attendance at the Inaugural Meeting were Mrs. J. A. Barclay, Ms. Peggy Billings, Dr. Hai Won Chang, Mrs. C. C. Choi, Dr. Myung Soon Oh, Mrs. F. M. Faist, Mrs. Mowat Fraser, Dr. Frances Fulton, Mrs. E. L. Hillman, Mrs. Maude Jensen, Mrs. Bessie Kim, Dr. Okgill Kim, Mr. Sae Sun Kim, Mrs. Wayne Lamb, Dr. James Laney, Mrs. James Laney, Mrs. W. Earl Ledden, Mr. P. William Lee, Mrs. W. W. McLendon, Mrs. John Norris, Rev. Henry Oh, Dr. Samuel Smith, Mrs. Charles Tillett, Dr. Hiram Weld, and Dr. Kilchai Yim.

The staff members were Mrs. Hilda Lee Dail, Mr. Moon Pyo Hong, and Mrs. Alva Love.

The organizing of the Foundation groups focused on area chapters, programs, campaign strategies, international student exchanges, faculty exchange processes, solicitations of donors from American businesses with interests in Korea, and the exploration of various foundations that provide grants. Church connections beyond the Methodist denomination were stressed to broaden the interdenominational, ecumenical dimension. The making of personal contacts with Korean Americans in churches, including Ewha graduates, was to be explored.

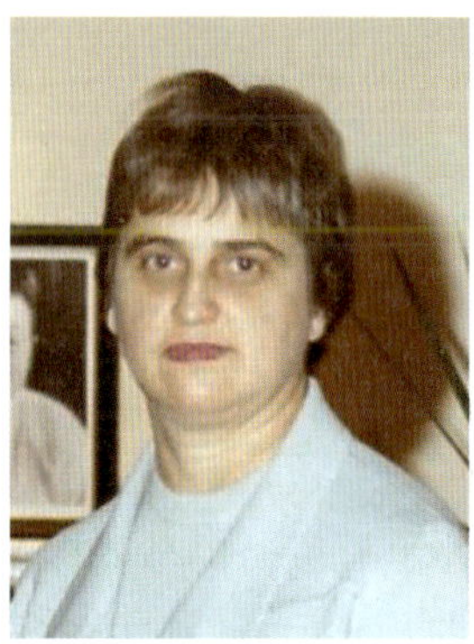

Inaugural Chair, IFEWU,
Miss Peggy Billings
[International Foundation Archives]

Mrs. Hilda Lee Dail was Executive Director for the initial International Foundation development for the period from February 1970 through September 1971. She had worked as a staff of the United Methodist Church. Mrs. Dail took a vacation trip on an African Safari tour in July 1970 and ran into Ms. Betty Hibben (later Dr. Betty Mitchell) as a roommate in a tree house accommodation. Mrs. Dail mentioned about her work as the Executive Director for the Foundation. Mrs. Hibben indicated how impressed she was by Dr. Helen Kim, having met her a year or two before in Chicago. After Mrs. Dail returned to New York, she mentioned about meeting Mrs. Hibben to the Foundation Executive Committee and recommended her as a possible President for the Foundation.

The new International Foundation worked on developing social networking through the mass media including video programs, full length films and brochures, updating the Ewha Room at Lake Junaluska, and distributing a *Helen's Last Words* leaflet sent with personal notes suggesting memorial gifts. The text of the leaflet appears in Appendix A.

An Ad-Interim Advisory Committee had several special meetings after the Inaugural Meeting of the Foundation Board of Directors held on April 15, 1970. Initially, the members were Ms. Peggy Billings, Mrs. Estelle Hillman, Mrs. Henrietta Gibson Ledden, Mr. Edward Poitras for Dr. Charles Germany, Dr. Samuel Smith, Dr. Kilchai K. Yim, Mrs. Hilda Lee Dail, Mr. Moon Pyo Hong, and Mrs. Alva Love. Meetings were held in September and December 1970 and in early 1971. The series of meetings dealt with the administrative budget, gifts, tax law interpretation, merger actions, transfer of funds, and many other issues related to the establishment and operation of the fledging organization.

At the Advisory Committee's December 17, 1970 meeting, Mrs. Betty Hibben's name was presented for consideration as President of the Foundation. It was moved that she be invited to become the President of the Foundation.

At the same meeting, the role and membership responsibilities of members of the Board of Directors were discussed and finalized. The following responsibilities were delineated:

1. Possession of a fundamental interest in the purpose of the Foundation.
2. Ability to attend Board meetings.
3. Contribution to the Board, either in work or in financial resources.
4. Willingness to represent Ewha in a geographical or organizational area.

The Advisory Committee, made up of Board members residing in the New York area, consisting of the President, Vice President, and two members of the former Cooperating Board (Mrs. E. L. Hillman and Mrs. Henrietta Gibson Ledden), was to meet when necessary to transact any business between Annual Meetings of the Board.

As of December 31, 1970, total receipts of $104,179 had been transferred from the Ewha Cooperating Board to the new Foundation, including the Pfeiffer Endowment, the Development Funds, Helen Kim Memorial Fund, Appenzeller Scholarship Fund, Harriet Morris Fund, Cassidy Scholarship Fund, Riverside Church Fund, Scholarship for Sun Sook Kim, Bequest of Miss Minnie Raab, Bequest of Miss Margaret Hiller and Legacy of Dr. Helen Kim, Appropriations of Board of World Mission, United Church of Canada, World Division of Prayers, Women's Division of the United Methodist Church, and others.

Starting on October 2, 1970, the Foundation began the transfer of funds to Ewha Womans University. The total amount sent to Ewha was $31,469 by December 31, 1970. These transactions marked the successful implementation of the International Foundation that had been created specifically to provide assistance to Ewha Womans University.

The International Foundation Comes into Being

The Year 1971 marked the end of the lengthy process of making the International Foundation a legal entity. The Foundation was registered in New York and obtained a new Charter in New York State. The Washington, DC area Foundation was disbanded. The Cooperating Board name was changed to the Foundation as were its Articles of Incorporation. The International Foundation Constitution and By-laws were established. They were essentially identical with those of the former Ewha Cooperating Board in North America. The titles of names of organizations were changed from Ewha Cooperating Board in North America to the International Foundation for Ewha Womans University, Inc.

The Foundation was structured as follows:

1. Executive Committee
2. Nominations Committee
3. Section on Promotional Planning including Operations, Program, Regional and Gifts Committees
4. Section on Public Relations including Hospitality and Publicity
5. Section on Inter-Agency Relationships including International Education and Cultural Exchange and Church Religious Affairs
6. Section on Finance including Scholarships, Budget, and Investment.

The First Annual Meeting of the Board of Directors, International Foundation for Ewha Womans University, Inc., was held on May 5-6, 1971 at the Statler Hilton Hotel in New York. Twenty-nine Board Members and two staff members participated. At the meeting, Ms. Peggy Billings, who had acted skillfully in her role chairing the organizational meetings to coordinate the merging of the two groups of members coming from the Ewha Cooperating Board and the Ewha Development Com-

Dr. Okgill Kim speaking at Foundation's Inaugural Meeting Banquet with Foundation President Betty Hibben to her right [International Foundation Archives]

mittee, introduced Mrs. Betty Hibben, the newly elected first President of the Foundation.

An important part of the First Annual Meeting was the awarding of citations by President Hibben to four individuals for their special contributions to the establishment of the Foundation. They were Ms. Peggy Billings, Prof. Margaret Forsyth, Dr. Estelle Hillman, and Dr. Henrietta Gibson Ledden.

Ms. Peggy Billings' citation summed up her critical role:

> *It has been her astute leadership during this formative period that has made it possible for the Foundation to come to this point in its history. She carried the responsibility of Chairmanship of the Foundation until the discovery of someone who could become its President. Thus in a very real sense Peggy is the mother of the Foundation.*

Prof. Margaret Forsyth, member of the Teacher's College, Columbia University faculty had become acquainted with Helen Kim during her graduate studies at Teacher's College. They shared mutual interests in the

YWCA and Ewha in the years that followed. Prof. Forsyth was one of the initial members of the Foundation, played an important role in its incorporation, and served for a while as its treasurer.

Dr. Henrietta Gibson Ledden, a longtime supporter and benefactor of Ewha (Gibson Hall was named after her father) was deeply involved in the creation of the International Foundation. She served as President of the Cooperating Board at one time, and according to her citation, "More than any other single American, Henrietta has gone out on the limb for Ewha." Her citation also read, "We simply could not exist today without your pioneering both in the past and in the present. You have the freshness of a crusader and we follow your firm step into the future, ..."

Dr. Estelle Hillman's ties with Ewha began when she was a member of the Board of Missions of the Methodist Church. She became a member of the Ewha Cooperating Board and was its President when the International Foundation was formed. She was especially helpful by taking on many responsibilities to make the Foundation an effective instrument to serve Ewha. She was described by a charter member of the Foundation as a towering leader for laying the organization's foundation. Her sense of humor and dedicated Christian spirit uplifted and inspired Board members.

The Foundation's Executive Committee members consisted of 12 persons including President Betty Hibben, Mr. Donald Warmkessel as Vice President, Mrs. Mowat Fraser as Vice President, Mrs. Wayne Lamb as Secretary, Mr. George Hergesheimer as Treasurer, Dr. Bumsun Lee as Associate Treasurer, Dr. Kilchai K. Yim, Dr. Hai Won Chang, Ms. Peggy Billings, Mrs. Estelle Hillman, Dr. Sam Smith, and Mrs. Kathryne Sears. Later other members were added, including Mrs. Henrietta Gibson Ledden and Bishop Hazen Werner.

The first meeting of the Executive Committee was held on September 27, 1971 at the Interchurch Center, 475 Riverside Drive, New York, to conduct the business of the Foundation. It was there that President Betty

Hibben displayed the certificate from the Internal Revenue Service declaring the legality for tax deductions to persons making contributions. In all, it took two years with much difficulty to complete the legal processes for the merger of the International Foundation for Ewha Womans University, Inc. with the Ewha Cooperating Board of North America, Inc. On March 3rd, 1972 the merger was certified by the Office of the Secretary of New York State and by the Recorder of Deeds of the District of Columbia on March 17, 1972.

"There Must Be a Way to Let the Splendor Out"

Mrs. Betty Seabury Hibben was from Glenview, Illinois and was a descendant of Samuel Seabury, the first Episcopalian Bishop in the United States and for whom the Seabury Western Theological Seminary in Evanston was named. Her mother was a Methodist, and her parents helped to build Berea College. She was a member of the Executive Committee of the World Service Council of the YWCA National Board, a member of the Executive Committee of the Women's Auxiliary of the Salvation Army and of the American Japanese Society. She was a member of the Board of Trustees of George Williams College. Although she was not involved in the initial establishment of the Foundation, she was destined to become one of its most significant builders. In 1976, during Ewha's 90th Anniversary Celebration, she was awarded an honorary doctorate degree in recognition of her outstanding contributions.

As mentioned earlier, Mrs. Hibben had met Dr. Helen Kim during a YWCA meeting in Glenview in 1969. Dr. Kim told Mrs. Hibben about Ewha University. [Interestingly, Ewha alumna Mrs. Shin Hyung Kim (Home Economics, 1949), active YWCA member, introduced Dr. Helen Kim to Mrs. Hibben at that meeting. She and her husband, Dr. John Young Song Kim, later served the Foundation as Board members. Mrs. Kim established a scholarship in 1984. Since 2003, a scholarship has

1st President, IFEWU, Dr. Betty Mitchell (a.k.a. Mrs. Betty Hibben) and Ewha President Okgill Kim [Ewha Archives]

been awarded every year to a student in the Department of Social Work.] Mrs. Hibben recalled asking Dr. Kim "if she would like to make a speech for Ewha in order to raise the funds at the meeting. Dr. Kim told me that she was not there to collect funds, but she was there to collect friends for Ewha. Her words left a deep impression on my mind, so I sent Dr. Kim a donation but I never received a reply from her." Dr. Kim passed away in February 1970 and probably never knew of the contribution. Mrs. Dail asked Mrs. Hibben to work on behalf of the newly created International Foundation. Mrs. Hibben responded positively by contributing $1,000 to the Foundation and began planning a visit to Ewha at her own expense in 1971.

The Nomination Committee members nominated Mrs. Betty Hibben to become President of the Foundation because of her energy, enthusiasm, experience, time, and potential source of financial resources. She accepted and served the Foundation as its president from 1971 to 1978.

In May 1971, Mrs. Betty Hibben visited Ewha Womans University in order to become acquainted with the faculty and the students. She was well received by the University and she fell in love with the University.

The University made a film, *Betty at Ewha*, which was shown many places in the U.S.

Mrs. Hibben was inspired by the students, faculty, and the ideals of Ewha. Her visit to Ewha helped to build greater understanding of the relationship between the Foundation and Ewha University. The path to the future for the Foundation to assist the progress of Ewha University became clearer to her. At the Board meeting on September 27, 1972, she gave a glowing report saying, "There Must Be a Way to Let the Splendor Out." The title was elegantly and thoughtfully drawn from poet Robert Browning's profound words:

> *There is an inmost center in us all, where truth abides in fullness; ... and, to know, rather consists in opening out a way where the imprisoned splendor may escape, than in effecting entry for a light supposed to be without.*

The Board of Directors of the International Foundation consisted of 35 members that were designated by the By-Laws of the Foundation. The goals of the Foundation were not limited to the fund-raising. They eventually evolved to include roles such as information services for international exchange programs for Ewha faculty enhancement in North America and for American students to pursue Asia cultural studies, as well as the purchasing and shipment of science and medical equipment and supplies, library books, and musical instruments for Ewha.

The first two years of the Foundation was a period devoted to defining the Foundation. Establishing its legal status as a tax-exempt organization was a frustrating and time-consuming process. Of utmost importance was the need to bring into alignment two disparate approaches to growing the Foundation. The Executive Director conceptualized and began implementing a several-year plan requiring substantial start-up financial investment. Others, including the University, had the expectation that the

Foundation would operate without deficit and produce tangible benefits almost immediately.

It was soon clear that funds were not available nor could debt be incurred by the Foundation to proceed through a several-year development phase. At the Advisory Committee meeting of September 27, 1971, in the presence of Ewha President Okgill Kim, drastic changes in the operation of the Foundation office were made to address the administrative budget crisis. The staff of three was reduced to one, with the one remaining being Mr. Moon Pyo Hong.

Mrs. Hilda Lee Dail's resignation as Executive Director was regretfully accepted as of September 30, 1971. Mr. Hong became the Executive Secretary for the Foundation, while continuing to help with the bookkeeping under the leadership of Mr. George Hergesheimer, Treasurer, and Dr. Bumsun Lee, Associate Treasurer. After Mr. Hergesheimer resigned on May 10, 1972, Dr. Lee became the Foundation Treasurer and Dr. Charles Germany became the Associate Treasurer.

The financial structure of the Foundation was thoroughly detailed and accounted for from 1971 until 2009 by Dr. Bumsun Lee. He was a graduate of Seoul National University and came to the U.S. in 1953 for graduate studies. He and his wife, Dr. Hyang Won Lee (Medicine, class of 1951), were members of the Ewha Development Committee. Dr. Helen Kim, while she was in New York in 1969, asked Dr. Bumsun Lee to look after development funds on behalf of Ewha. His faithful voluntary service resulted in Dr. Lee being the longest serving officer and Board member of the Foundation.

The Board decided to create an Investment Committee. It initially consisted of Mrs. Betty Hibben, Mrs. Henrietta G. Ledden, Dr. Bumsun Lee, Mrs. S. E. McCreless, Mrs. Kathryne Sears, Mr. Donald Warmkessel, and Dr. Kilchai K.Yim.

The management of the Foundation's portfolio was turned over to Kidder, Peabody and Co. of Chicago and the custody of the Foundation's securities was left with the Irving Trust Company. The Irving Trust Company had custody of the Ewha Cooperating Board's securities for many years.

Mr. Moon Pyo Hong, as the Executive Director of the Foundation, fulfilled many responsibilities, including fundraising, bookkeeping, corresponding, coordinating the events of Foundation activities, and facilitating between Ewha and other institutions for exchange programs for students and professors, purchasing and shipping educational equipment and facilities to Ewha University.

The Foundation during the 1970s worked on several challenging projects to assist Ewha University. This was during a time Ewha was experiencing provocative restrictions by the government as it strived to create a university on par with international standards. In order to progress towards a world-class university, the goal of Ewha University was to emphasize curriculum development and faculty enhancement.

Dr. Okgill Kim, the eighth President of Ewha University, furthered the ideals of internationalization through partnering with the Foundation to connect with other Christian universities in Asia, focusing on cooperative, international research, and faculty exchange. The International Summer School programs and the summer program in Asia Studies at Ewha were initiated.

In 1971, the office of the International Foundation was asked to assist the International Summer School in Asian Studies at Ewha University, initiated by Prof. David Suh, Dean of the College of Liberal Arts. The summer school program was designed for high school students who were the children of Korean Americans and Koreans living in the U.S. The Foundation office helped promote the program in the churches and schools in the United States and assisted in processing applicants. In later years, the International Summer School program focused on university students.

For the promotion of Ewha University internationally and for fundraising, the Ewha Womans University's Glee Club toured the U.S. in 1972. Dr. Frances Fulton, a missionary and professor of voice in Ewha's Music Department, accompanied the group of 42 voices. They gave performances at the John F. Kennedy Center of the Performing Arts in Washington, DC, the Lincoln Center in New York, eight colleges and universities, and churches, including the First United Methodist Church of Evanston, IL. On the U.S. west coast, they performed in San Francisco and Seattle. The Glee Club was highly applauded by the U.S. media (including the *New York Times*) and by Ewha alumnae.

In 1973, the Ewha Alumnae Entertainment Troup of Korea toured the U.S. presenting a "Korean Evening of Music and Dance" under the directorship of Dr. Kim Yong-yi, the former Dean of Ewha's College of Music. The group was composed of two folk dancers, a kayakeum player, a flutist, a pianist, and two vocalists. They gave 12 performances between March 7 and March 29. They presented their program in Boston, New York, Philadelphia, Baltimore, Washington, DC, Cleveland, Detroit, Chicago, Minneapolis, Seattle, San Francisco, and Los Angeles. Their estimated total audience was 6,950, and their fundraising generated more than $16,000.

The Entertainment Troup was hosted by Ewha alumnae during their U.S. tour, with expenses largely covered by Ewha alumnae. For example, Mrs. Jai Kang Song, '57 Chemistry major graduate and a leader of the local Ewha Alumnae Association in Minnesota, worked with others to make room and board arrangements in alumnae's homes in Bloomingdale, MN for the group when it came to perform at a local church. The Association raised $1,000 for the Minnesota Ewha Scholarship Fund. A crucial benefit of these Ewha Alumnae performances in the various cities was the creation or strengthening of local Ewha Alumnae Chapters throughout the U.S. Additionally, they showcased and promoted the talents of Ewha graduates while bolstering pride among alumnae.

The Foundation expanded its fundraising efforts in 1972 by sending out Christmas appeals to 1,000 friends of Ewha and 1,000 Ewha alumnae who lived in the U.S. The mass mailing resulted in gifts received from 3.5% of the mail recipients.

The Foundation soon saw the establishment of endowments set up for scholarships, such as the permanent Laura Mae Ehman Memorial Scholarship Fund for Home Economics, the Seabury Library Fund for the Ewha Graduate School, the Betty Mitchell Scholarship Fund, and the Kilchai Yim Fund.

The permanent and special funds under custody at Irving Trust Company totaled $455,111 at the end of 1971. The receipts of gifts in 1972 was $18,381. By 1976, the receipt of contributions had significantly increased to $150,000.

[In 1972, Mrs. Betty Hibben became Mrs. Betty S. Mitchell. Henceforth, she will be identified in this publication as Dr. Betty S. Mitchell, to also recognize her receipt of an honorary Doctorate of English Literature at the 90th Anniversary Celebration of Ewha on May 31, 1976.]

The Foundation, led by Dr. Betty S. Mitchell, in partnership with the University, led by President Okgill Kim, established a stable financial base for the Foundation with support for Foundation administration, endowment growth (including the establishment of the first student scholarship endowments), and support to Ewha.

In 1976, a special grant was received from the Canadian International Development Agency for a "Maple Leaf" Christian Children's Service Center at Ewha, made possible through Mr. Frank Wilsmith, a Foundation Board member from Canada. The Foundation became even more international when the Canadian Board of the Christian Children's Fund donated $40,000 for a Children's Welfare Center building at Ewha. The World Division of Global Ministries, Canadian Church also helped.

The International Foundation was being provided office space by the United Board for Christian Higher Education in Asia in the Interchurch Center, Riverside Drive, New York. Shanghai Women's Medical College belonged to the United Board. Because China had come under communist rule, funds of Shanghai Women's Medical College residing in the United Board were given to the International Foundation. According to Mr. Moon Pyo Hong, the Shanghai Women's Medical College Board contributed $100,000 towards a nurses' dormitory for Ewha's Medical School.

The mid-1970s was a challenging period in Korea. University students, including Ewha students, strongly resisted authoritarianism and military rule. At the same time Korea had a great need for trained human resources for the rapid industrialization resulting largely from the economic benefits to Korea arising from the Vietnam War. Ewha University urgently sought financial assistance to provide educational opportunities enabling greater numbers of young women to join in the country's development. The Foundation provided indispensable support for Ewha during this period of rapid and chaotic nation building.

The Foundation acquired medical supplies and equipment at very nominal cost. The Church World Service assisted the Foundation in shipping of the medical supplies and equipment, some of which was procured from U.S. Government surplus. A total of 216 cartons with contents having an estimated market value of $122,000 were shipped in 1972. The Interchurch Medical Assistance, Inc. (IMA) helped procure two new X-Ray machines for the Ewha University Medical School. [IMA represents some of the largest U.S. Protestant relief and development agencies in procuring and dispensing essential medical products and services for overseas emergency, health, and development programs that serve the poor.]

For the College of Music, a harpsichord was donated by Dr. Betty S. Mitchell and a Baldwin organ was given by Mrs. Poyoung Lee Kim (a '56 graduate of Ewha's Music Department) who lived in New York. Library books, supplies and microfilm reader for Ewha Library and a refrigerator circulator for the College of Pharmacy were sent through the

Foundation. Coordination and the processes for shipping were managed and handled by Mr. Moon Pyo Hong.

The Foundation's Committee of International Educational and Cultural Exchange promoted the Ewha International Summer School program by advertising and processing application information. The Committee was involved in two unique activities. As described earlier, one started in 1971 and focused on bringing American students to Ewha to learn about Asia culture and society in a six-week summer program. The Foundation office conducted the application process for the prospective students.

The second activity dealt with the essential role of the Foundation to assist Ewha University in providing enhancement opportunities for Ewha faculty to upgrade their scholarly and professional competencies. One of the many contributions that Dr. Betty S. Mitchell directed during her leadership was connecting the International Foundation with the Seabury Foundation for this purpose.

The Seabury Foundation

Financial support by the Seabury Foundation was initiated through the efforts of Dr. Betty Mitchell. In 1973, the Seabury Foundation contributed $11,000 towards the administrative fund of the Foundation and $5,000 to the Betty Mitchell Scholarship Fund.

The Seabury Foundation was established by Rev. Charles Ward and Louise Lovett Seabury in 1947 in Chicago. Dr. Betty Seabury Mitchell's full name reveals the family connection. The early interests of the Seabury Foundation included support for the major cultural and civic institutions in Chicago, and educational opportunities for those who could not afford them. Later, it expanded its interests to providing support to the International Foundation and Ewha.

The funding from the Seabury Foundation helped cover administrative costs while the International Foundation was making the essential transition to becoming a self-sufficient organization. Later, the Seabury Foundation gave annual grants for scholarships and the purchasing of books for the Ewha University Library. Of truly major significance was the funding of a Visiting Scholars Program for Ewha faculty enhancement. Dr. Shin In-ryung, President Kim Sun-uk, Dr. Park Dong-ki, Dr. Kim Ho-soon, Dr. Paik Myung-hee, Prof. Kim Sei-young, Dr. Chang Pilwha, and 28 other Ewha professors received grants from the Visiting Scholars program for advanced education and research in the U.S. since 1972. The Seabury Foundation Visiting Scholars Program continues; $18,000 was available in 2011 for two grants.

In addition to the assistance already mentioned, the Seabury Foundation provided a one-time grant for the development of fund-raising promotional materials to encourage gifts through various avenues.

Moving Forward: 1979–1990

During the 1970s, the Foundation's Board of Directors under Dr. Betty Mitchell's leadership worked diligently to establish a permanent self-sustaining organization while simultaneously delivering critically needed assistance to the rapidly maturing Ewha Womans University. Again, numerous individuals in Korea and from around the world made contributions large and small to the growing momentum of a river of faith that had begun its flow about a century earlier. Their efforts, combined with those who came before them, confirmed Dr. Mitchell's assertion made after her first visit to Ewha that, "There must be a way to let the splendor out." While major accomplishments had been made, Dr. Helen Kim's use of words from the same poet (Robert Browning) Dr. Mitchell had drawn from continued to resonate; "The best is yet to be."

The organizational structure of the Foundation was put in place during Dr. Betty Mitchell's tenure as president. Mrs. Kathryne Sears succeeded Dr. Mitchell as the President of the Foundation in 1979. President Sears further institutionalized the structure during her service, ensuring stability and permanence. She was a Missionary Personnel Secretary for the Methodist Board of Missions and became involved with Ewha Cooperating Board in North America during 1947-1970. She was a charter member of the Foundation and served as a Board member from 1971 to 1994.

2nd President, IFEWU,
Mrs. Kathryne Sears
[International Foundation Archives]

During President Sears' tenure, the Board strengthened the organizational structure by the study and revision of the Constitution and the By-Laws of the Foundation.

During this time period, four bequests were received from the friends of Ewha: Dr. S. E. McCreless for his memorial scholarship fund, Mabel I. Tilton Estate ($5,000), Miss Christine Ayars Estate ($1,000), Miss Ailene J. Wilson Estate ($5,000), and Dr. Velma Maynor Estate ($2,000). Also, the Chosen Mission in Erie, Pennsylvania provided the Ewha University Hospital with medical equipment donated by the American Sterilizer Company worth $34,682. The equipment was shipped with the assistance of Interchurch Medical Assistance, Inc. (IMA).

Part 5

New Frontiers and the Centennial Celebration: 1981-1989

The Foundation Helps Our Ewha to Become a Mecca of Learning

The Foundation's second decade was a time when Ewha Womans University faced special challenges. In 1980, Mrs. Mamie Lee Finger was elected as the Foundation President. She was a visionary fund raiser with professional organizational skills and a dynamic promoter for support of Christian education for women through Ewha Womans University. Benefiting from an already solid base, her leadership set clear and systematic directions for the Foundation that reaped critically needed benefits for Ewha.

Mrs. Mamie Lee Finger made her first speech as President at the Foundation's 10th Annual meeting at the Hyatt Regency Hotel in Los Angeles, California on November 7, 1981:

> *... we come to the Annual Meeting with good feelings of accomplishment we have made together. There is also excitement as we look togeth-*

er at challenges and opportunities before us. As we celebrated Ewha's 95th birthday in May, moving on toward the Centennial, it has become important to reclaim wide support constituency. Of prime importance is to publicize Ewha so that people who are not acquainted with our school will become aware of this strong and renowned University.

Mrs. Mamie Lee Finger graduated summa cum laude and Phi Beta Kappa from Agnes Scott College and was the wife of pastor, Navy chaplain, college president and Bishop H. Ellis Finger, Jr. She took part in activities relating to the history and archives of the United Methodist Church, especially women's history.

She served as the President of the Foundation from 1980 through 1986 when Ewha University was in need of critical assistance while coping with the threat to academic freedom during the military control of the Korean government. However, Mrs. Finger's leadership was encapsulated in the description that she was an indefatigable and invaluable fundraiser. During her term the Foundation's portfolio more than doubled in value. During her term the Foundation contributed over $1,000,000 for the new library building and for library books. The highlight of President Finger's contributions to the operation of the Foundation was the initiation of an endowment for administration funds. When Mrs. Finger's husband, Bishop Finger, retired in 1984, the Holston Conference (Knoxville) made a generous donation to Ewha, which Mrs. Finger matched the following year. At the Centennial Celebration of Ewha, May 30, 1986, she was honored with an honorary doctorate.

3rd President, IFEWU,
Mrs. Mamie Lee Finger
[International Foundation Archives]

During the 1980s, Ewha Womans University faced continuing crises and arduous challenges. The continued threats by the government and student political actions, including demonstrations against the military dictatorship, created a difficult climate for pursuing dreams of excellence in higher education. For example, the Ministry of Education imposed a quota system on universities as of July 30, 1980 requiring them to admit 130% of the usual freshman enrollment and to fail 30% of them after four years of competing with their peers. This and other imposed policies during a period when the number of students at Ewha increased from 10,000 to 20,000 created crises and challenges related to limited building space, curriculum, and teaching. Such policies hampered the quality of education at Ewha as well as at other Korean universities.

In spite of the challenges to its orderly growth, the spirit of Ewha Womans University moved forward with its goal to become a premier university under the resilient and forward looking leadership of President Chung Ii-sook (1979-1990). Under President Chung, Ewha reaffirmed its commitment to overcome the challenges it faced and to transform the University into the mecca of learning its leadership had long envisioned. President Chung decisively presented and implemented a plan to grow Ewha into a "center of learning and research-focused university."[38] The dreams to fulfill included greater internationalism focus, academic research facilities, funds for research, more buildings for the increased student enrollment, more scholarships, and having the largest library in Korea, the Centennial Library with one million volumes and a computer lab and cataloging system. During her tenure as President of Ewha, Dr. Chung brought these dreams to reality.

The economic situation in the U.S. at the time did not provide a favorable fundraising climate for the Foundation. Among other factors taking their toll on the U.S. economy were the significant and lasting impacts of the 1973 oil embargo. However, the tenacious strength of Mrs. Finger and Foundation Board members harnessed much needed support for President Chung's drive to advance Ewha as a mecca of learning. They

Ewha's 9th President Dr. Chung Ii-sook [Ewha Archives]

gave emphasis to their efforts by describing Ewha as "*Our Ewha!*"

Ewha President Chung, at the Twelfth Annual Meeting of the Foundation Board at Marriot Hotel in Chicago on November 5th, 1982, expressed her deep gratitude for the assistance the Foundation was delivering during the very difficult time she was experiencing as she worked towards building Ewha into a premier university.

President Chung asked for the prayers, concern, and dedicated assistance of the International Foundation in helping Ewha into the bright future. She was gratified for the various pieces of equipment and supplies that had been shipped to Ewha to meet the special needs of research and the University Hospital, for the Speech and Hearing Center which had been supported by the United Church of Canada, the Social Welfare Center which was sponsored by the Canadian Children's Fund, the dual sponsorship of the United Board of Christian Higher Education in Asia and the United Methodist church for development of the Korea Women's Institute, and the financial aid that had been given for faculty enhancement abroad through Seabury Foundation grants.

In November 1985, at the 16th Annual Board Meeting of the International Foundation in Gaithersburg, Maryland, President Chung Ii-sook spoke of the historical meanings of Ewha on the occasion of the upcoming Centennial Year of its founding. She summarized them by stating that Ewha can be said to be a record of truth to clarify the glory of God, of liberating those under oppression, and of intellectual victory of liberating humanity. This past history, she reflected, sets the stage for the future. She then proceeded to outline the ideal perspective of Ewha for the coming future. These included Ewha playing a role in the actualization of peace and reconciliation and the educating of women professionally competent with a full sense toward the 21st century of the highly "electronized" intellectual world. President Chung then voiced a new role for Ewha:

> *I would like to project a tentative possibility of opening the door for the third world. ... This transformation of the role of Ewha would naturally open a new humanitarian possibility for the women of the third world and it would be the first forward step for Ewha toward the realization of an ideal world where spiritual values and the material abundance would be united."*

She then announced steps being undertaken at the time to make the vision a reality. She ended by saying,

> *We believe these attempts would be stepping stones for the higher advancement of the status of Ewha* ***from the receiving university to a giving university***.[39]

With this pronouncement, Ewha was serving notice that its mission to enlighten, educate and empower women was expanding beyond Korea's borders, giving new breadth and depth to its *River of Faith*.

Laying Systematic Networking

In 1981, International Foundation Board members, under the leadership of Mrs. Finger, stepped up their activities promoting Ewha through systematic networking and fundraising. The focus was on Ewha's Centennial Celebration to be held in 1986. Public relations and resource development for the Foundation were addressed. The office of Vice President for Resource Development was established, and Dr. Kilchai K. Yim was selected to fill the position. The Annual Board Meeting was expanded to two days to more fully conduct the business of the Foundation. The first day was devoted to the Executive Board Meeting and Annual Meeting of the Board. The second day was designed for Committee meetings. The first Foundation newsletter, entitled *Ewha Centennial News*, was issued and distributed to the friends and graduates of Ewha living in the U.S. and Canada.

Showing its seriousness to assist Ewha, the Foundation Board identified an ambitious list of 18 special tasks which it proceeded to undertake to promote fundraising for the Centennial Celebration. They were: 1) Contacting corporations with branch offices and industries in Korea, 2) Securing guidelines from various U.S. foundations to apply for grants, 3) Cultivating and encouraging Ewha alumnae to establish local chapters for fundraising, 4) Enlarging Foundation Board memberships, 5) Contacting former Board members, 6) Urging Board members to make personal contacts with the potential donors, 7) Exploring the promotion of elder hostels, 8) Seeking to have wider geographical representation on the Board, 9) Putting larger emphasis on fundraising, 10) Increasing the Ewha Alumnae mailing list for solicitation of Funds, 11) Electing Board member who can attract large gifts, 12) Enlarging the program and use of the Chorus and Dance Group, 13) Preparing and publicizing a list of the needs for the Centennial Library, 14) Offering more leadership training opportunities for service in third world countries, 15) Working toward more active exchange programs for students who would go to Ewha for International Summer Studies and a faculty exchange program for updating professional and academic research, 16) Working toward the establishment of new alumnae chapters, 17) Encouraging a closer relationship between the Board and the alumnae, and, 18) Setting up a plan for using the telephone in fundraising.

Dedication of Dr. Kilchai K. Yim to Partner with Alumnae Groups

Dr. Kilchai K. Yim was an Ewha alumna of special distinction measured in terms of her faithfulness, hard work, financial contributions, and leadership in the efforts leading up to and following the formation of the International Foundation.

Dr. Yim was born on 18 February 1911. She graduated in 1933 from Ewha College's English Department. She went to Japan in 1935 and studied medicine at the Tokyo Imperial Women Medical College, from which she graduated in 1941. She returned to Korea and completed her internship and residency at Kyungsung (Seoul) Imperial Medical School, receiving a Doctor of Medicine degree in 1945. As a physician, she served as director of the Obstetrics and Gynecology Department, Ewha Womans University Hospital from 1945 to 1949.

Dr. Yim came to the U.S. in April 1949 for medical training at the University of Michigan and then undertook an internship and residency at St. Catherine's Hospital in Brooklyn, New York from 1950 to 1955. She studied at New York Medical College for two years. She practiced obstetrics and gynecological medicine from 1960 to 1986 in New York.

Dr. Yim served as the President of the Ewha Womans University Alumnae Association of the New York Metropolitan Area from 1964 to 1967. She was a member of the Ewha Cooperating Board of North America from 1967 to 1971. She played a leading role for the Ewha Decade Development Committee in New York in order to assist the vision of Dr. Helen Kim. She was a charter member of the International Foundation. She served as the Foundation's Vice

Dr. Kilchai K. Yim
[International Foundation Archives]

President from 1981 to 2002. Ewha Womans University awarded Dr. Kilchai K. Yim an honorary doctorate in 1976. In 1997 she was recognized as a *Distinguished Ewhaian* by the University. In 2003, the Foundation honored her with a plaque for her love for and devotion to Ewha and the Foundation.

As the Foundation's Vice President, Dr. Yim played an invaluable role in promoting public relations events and encouraging Ewha alumnae and their families to participate in the fundraising. In 1973, she led the Foundation's sponsoring of the tour of the Ewha Music and Dance Group to Honolulu, San Francisco, Los Angeles, Dallas, Atlanta, Knoxville, Chicago, Washington, DC, Baltimore, Philadelphia, New York Area, Boston, and Hicksville, New York.

Dr. Yim strongly believed in building International Foundation endowments. From her perspective, a major reason for the Foundation's existence is to ensure financial support for Ewha as needs and emergencies emerge, and endowments can contribute heavily to making that happen. She contributed to endowments including those for the Foundation's Endowment Fund for Fiscal Operation, the Mokdong Hospital Endowment, and for the Dr. Kilchai Yim Scholarship Endowment. She contributed $50,000 towards a chapel in Mokdong Hospital.

Dr. Kilchai Yim remained engaged in the International Foundation until her passing on February 10, 2012, just one week short of her 101st birthday.

Fundraising for the Centennial Memorial Library: 1982–1986

A second tour of the Ewha Music and Dance Group was directed towards encouraging Ewha alumnae to form local chapters. These chapters were urged to raise funds to assist Ewha. The chapter formation created a networking mechanism that strengthened the Foundation's fundraising efforts. The contributions received by the Foundation reached $189,500 by 1982 including $38,418 that was raised by the alumnae groups in 13 cities to be directed towards the Centennial Library. The successful fund-raising confirmed that the growing number of Ewha alumnae in North America was an emerging source of support for Ewha.

Dr. Okgill Kim, accompanied by her brother Yonsei University Prof. Donggill Kim, made a speaking tour of local alumnae chapters in major U.S. cities in 1983. The tour's primary goal was to promote the development of Ewha Alumnae Chapters while encouraging fundraising for Ewha.

The emphasis on public relations and fundraising had momentous impacts on the development and growth of alumnae chapters in North America. As an example, Dr. Soon Ja Choi, the 1982 President of Ewha Womans University Alumnae Association of Chicago and Mr. Joseph Yi, a Foundation Board member, organized a banquet for fundraising at the Foundation's Annual Board meeting in Chicago. They dedicated the meeting to raising funds for the Centennial Library. Some 420 guests participated in the November 6, 1982 banquet. As a result, the Chicago group pledged $20,000 for the Centennial Library fund.

The tours by Dr. Okgill Kim, Dr. Donggill Kim, and the Ewha Music and Dance group, as well as a speech given by Dr. Chung Ii-sook for the New York Ewha alumnae association, not only promoted Ewha University but also encouraged many alumnae to contribute funds for the Centennial Library and other Ewha causes.

All the heightened activity spurred Foundation Board members to participate more heavily in contributing to the Centennial Memorial Library project. Most notably, Dr. Betty Mitchell pledged and contributed $200,000 toward the construction of the building and the purchase of library books. She continued to assist with another $300,000 for computerizing the Library, making it the first of its kind in Korea.

One of the significant achievements of the Foundation was the concerted drive to celebrate the Ewha University Centennial by funding the Centennial Memorial Library. From outside the Ewha community and its own International Foundation, the International Foundation of Butler, New Jersey awarded a grant of $250,000 to the International Foundation for Ewha Womans University towards the purchase of books and furnishings for the Centennial Memorial Library. The grant was made through the request of Mrs. Finger and given to honor Dr. Hurst R. Anderson. Dr. Anderson was an outstanding civic, educational and church leader. He served as President of Hamline University in St. Paul, Minnesota and the American University in Washington, DC. He also served on the World Methodist Council and Executive College of General Conferences of the Methodist Church. Both Dr. and Mrs. Anderson were classmates and good friends of Dr. Helen Kim at Ohio Wesleyan University in the 1920's.

The successful fundraising was met with jubilation by the International Foundation, the leaders of Ewha including President Chung Ii-

The Centennial Library [Ewha Archives]

Ewha and International Foundation leadership celebrating opening of Centennial Library
[Ewha Archives]

sook and Dr. Okgill Kim, and the alumnae and friends of Ewha.

The joyous Ewha Centennial celebration took place in Seoul on May Day 1986, with 185 persons from the U.S. and Canada attending, including Board members and Ewha alumnae. Mr. Moon Pyo Hong made the travel arrangements for the group. It was at the Centennial convocation that Mrs. Finger received an honorary doctorate and Mr. Hong was awarded a special citation.

During the 1980 to 1986 time period, the organizational structure of the Foundation was consolidated by legal documents. The By-Laws were updated and local Ewha Alumnae Chapters were created and fostered to develop partnerships to assist Ewha University through the Foundation. The Foundation promoted the image and needs of Ewha through publications such as brochures and newsletters, and through the distribution of materials through churches to cultivate understanding about Korea.

Miss Dorothy B. Smith
[International Foundation Archives]

A total of $688,700 was raised for the Centennial Library building and $309,850 for books. In addition, another $151,000 for library books came from the Dorothy Smith Foundation from a bequest of the late Dorothy Smith.

Dorothy B. Smith was born in 1901 in Moundridge, Kansas, the daughter of an insurance man and land owner. Smith taught in an English-speaking school in Seoul, Korea for one year. She was a friend of Harriet Morris and Marian Conrow, both missionaries to Ewha. She was impressed by Ewha and bequeathed to Ewha Womans University through the International Foundation one-fourth of her estate and two-fifths of the mineral rights of land with gas wells. The Finance Committee of the Foundation sold the real estate which provided the contribution for the Centennial Library books but retained the mineral rights. The three gas wells located in Grant County, Kansas were still earning income in 2011.

The Alice R. Appenzeller Award was endowed and advance special funds of $9,400 were raised for the Speech and Hearing Center. The Permanent Fund of the Investment portfolio grew from a 1980 value of $677, 940 to a value exceeding $1,500,000 in 1987.

At the Fall 1986 Annual Board Meeting, Mrs. Estelle Hillman, a Board member and past president of the Ewha Cooperating Board in North America, paid tribute to the accomplishments of Mamie Lee Finger's leadership from 1980 to 1986:

The loving care that Mamie Lee has shown to each member of this Board has welded us into a strong and loyal body, caring for each member and for the institution we serve. She has set a remarkable record of complete dedication and faithfulness, and we can do no less than pledge to her and to ourselves our continued dedication and faithfulness to Ewha Womans University.[40]

One of the great accomplishments of the Foundation during the 1980s was connecting with greater numbers of Ewha alumnae as partners. This resulted largely from the joint endeavors to reach the special goals of providing support to build and equip the Centennial Memorial Library as part of the Ewha Centennial Celebration and to strengthen Ewha as a mecca of learning. This work was another triumphant symbol of the power of prayer and the compassion of friends and alumnae in North America, as acclaimed by President Alice Appenzeller when Pfeiffer Hall was opened in 1935.

Into Ewha's Second Century: 1987-1989

The 18th Annual Meeting of the Foundation Board was held in November 1987 at the Royce Hotel at La Guardia Airport, Queens, New York. Mrs. Susan Ruby Lamb, the new President of the Foundation, commented on the beginning of Ewha's second century:

It is not only the beginning of a new year but the beginning of a second century in the life of Ewha Womans University. During the past year we have celebrated in a magnificent manner the Centennial of Ewha's first one hundred years of notable achievements and noting the progress from the beginning with one pupil and one teacher to an enrollment of almost 20,000 students today."[41]

Mrs. Susan R. Lamb was a member of Ewha Womans University Cooperating Board in North America, member of the Ewha Decade Development Committee, charter member of the International Foundation, and Secretary of the Foundation who impeccably kept the records of the

4th President, IFEWU,
Mrs. Susan Ruby Lamb
[International Foundation Archives]

Foundation. Along with her husband, Rev. Wayne Lamb, she went to Korea in 1960 on an evangelizing mission led by Dr. Harry Denman. She and her friends and former colleagues of Dr. Denman did fundraising for the Harry Denman Memorial Fund for the Ewha Centennial Memorial Library. She shared a long journey of friendship with Dr. Helen Kim.

Mrs. Lamb had been a leader of the United Methodist women in Memphis and throughout Tennessee, Dean of the School of Missions, and Conference President in Memphis. She was awarded an honorary doctorate degree from Lambuth College in Jackson, Tennessee.

Mrs. Lamb and other friends and alumnae of Ewha continued their united dedication for the development of Ewha through the Foundation. They included Dr. Mitchell serving as the Chair of the Committee on International Educational and Culture Exchange, Mrs. Finger as the Chair of the Special Gifts Committee, Mrs. Hillman as the Vice President and member of the Committee on Nominations, Dr. Kilchai Yim as the Vice President and member of the Committee on Finance, Mrs. Kathryne B. Sears serving as the Chair of the Committee on Finance, Dr. Hai Won Chang as the Chair of the Committee on Nominations, and Dr. Bumsun Lee on the Finance Committee, and Mr. Moon Pyo Hong, as Executive Director, long providing support implementing Board actions. Mrs. Sears and Mrs. Hillman had faithfully served for four decades since the creation of the Ewha Cooperating Board in North America.

At the 15th Annual Board Meeting in November 1984, a Special Endowment Fund for Fiscal Operation was established by the Foundation president to give the organization a stabilized operation. The earnings from the fund are used for the operating budget at the discretion of the Finance Committee and the Board. An endowment of $255,000 for administrative support was established to ensure the orderly continuity of the Foundation. Among the endowment contributions was $100,000 given by Dr. Betty Mitchell. Contributions to the endowment were made by Mrs. Mamie Lee Finger and Mrs. Eunice Beane. The McCreless Foundation donated $50,000 in 1987. Dr. Kilchai Yim initially contributed $10,000 in 1971 to the Kilchai Yim Fund I, to meet the fiscal crisis in 1971-1972. This Kilchai Yim Fund I reached its goal of $100,000 in the year 2000. The Fiscal Operation of the Foundation was to be self-supporting, largely by generosity and vision of these contributors and the assistance of the Board of Global Ministries of the United Methodist Church. This Board has provided a Foundation office for many years for nominal rent.

The Ewha Centennial Afterglow

"Its music in my heart I bore, long after it was heard no more."
William Wordsworth, *The Solitary Reaper*

After the magnificent Ewha Centennial celebration, the enthusiasm and spirit of the event gave lasting momentum to Foundation activity promoting Ewha and fundraising. Presentations about Ewha were given to a variety of church circles and civic groups. One example of particular interest was the follow-up that took place in Wichita, Kansas. Wichita is a special city for Ewha as Ms. Harriet Morris, missionary and professor of home economics at Ewha who had great love for Ewha, came from Wichita. It was also the place Dr. Helen Kim had called her second home.

Twelve Methodists from Wichita, Kansas had journeyed to Seoul to participate in the Ewha Centennial Celebration. They continued the celebration with "Our Love for Ewha" which took "wings" in the heart of

First United Methodist Church in Wichita. In honor of Ms. Morris, the Wichita church contributed $12,000 to the Foundation.

In the afterglow of the Centennial celebration, a wide variety of individual endowments were created or given additions, such as the Helen K. Kim Endowment, the Appenzeller Endowment, The Katherine Crane Fund, College of Nursing Fund, Estelle Hillman Scholarship Fund, Chun Hi and Joseph Crivello Fund, Shin Hyung Kim Scholarship Fund, Heeyul Lee Cho Scholarship Fund, the Harry and Harriet Kassop Scholarship Fund, and the Choung Cha Cho Scholarship Fund for the College of Medicine.

An ambitious fundraising campaign was conceived by the Chicago Alumnae Association under the leadership of Foundation Board member Dr. Soon Ja Choi for the purpose of growing an endowment to provide continuing education opportunities for Ewha faculty members (eventually it was combined with the Helen Kim Memorial Fund.) The campaign was organized around speaking engagements by Dr. Okgill Kim in the spring of 1989.

Dr. Soon Ja Choi and fellow Chicagoan and Foundation Board member Mr. Joseph Choong Sik Yi underwrote the costs of Dr. Okgill Kim's fund-raising tour. The zeal of Dr. Choi and Mr. Yi greatly impacted the networking among the Ewha alumnae in the U.S. and Canada. Dr. Choi, who was on the Foundation's Committee of Promotion and Public Relations, was a fervent activist for cultivating Ewha alumnae to participate in fundraising. Mr. Yi married into the Ewha family as his wife Soong Ok Yi was an Ewha alumnae. Mr. Yi became affectionately called an "Ewha's elder brother" among the alumnae because of his long service

Dr. Soon Ja Choi [International Foundation Archives]

Mr. Joseph C. Yi [International Foundation Archives]

as a Foundation Board member.

The circulation of the Foundation Newsletter, *Ewha News*, was increased to 2,000 copies to reach greater numbers of potential donors and friends of Ewha.

The Ewha Summer International School for 1987 was widely promoted and had record enrollment. Mr. Hong, received and processed 158 applicants from throughout the U.S. A total of 124 students participated.

Part 6

The New Era Growing with Hope and Faith: 1980-1995

Increasing Constituencies for the Foundation

From the late 1980s and onward, the Foundation made solid advances in the numbers and value of endowments and contributions. The leadership of Ewha and the Foundation worked closely to inspire Ewha alumnae in the U.S. and Canada to join as partners in the quest of growing Ewha into a mecca of learning of world class quality.

An example of the University and the Foundation working for the same common goal was an address delivered by Dr. Okgill Kim, President Emerita and Chair of the Board of Trustees of Ewha Womans University, at the 18th Annual International Foundation Board Meeting Dinner at the Royce Hotel at La Guardia Airport, New York on November 7, 1987. The dinner played a dual role by also being a fundraising event for the Ewha Centennial Library Book Fund hosted by the Ewha University Alumnae Association of the New York Metropolitan Area. Dr. Okgill Kim spoke:

Ewha, founded in the most critical period of Korea's recent history, has grown in crises with faith and hope ... I find the unshaking foundation of Ewha's educational philosophy in our founding mother's declaration of 1888. ... Mary F. Scranton wrote to the Christian audience at home in 1888 that the purpose of Ewha education is not to make Korean girls Americans but "better Koreans." ... "We want Korea to be proud of Korean things, and more, that it is a perfect Korea through Christ and his teachings. ... the spirit of our Christian education at Ewha is for the "one course of humble service" to the "mass of Korean women crying out for help." Our educational purpose is the emancipation of women in Korea and we stand firmly on the side of the poor and oppressed women of Korea as Jesus Christ himself stood firmly on the side of the people, and died for the salvation of the poor and helpless people of the world.[42]

In April 1989, Dr. Okgill Kim returned to the U.S. to make speeches at local Ewha Alumnae Chapters as part of the fundraising campaign initiated by the Chicago Alumnae Association and promoted by Foundation Board members such as Dr. Soon Ja Choi and Mr. Joseph Yi. The goal was to raise funds for construction of the new teaching hospital complex in Mok-Dong in southwest Seoul and also for the Helen Kim Endowment for the Faculty Exchange program under which renowned scholars are invited to lecture at Ewha University.

Dr. Okgill Kim [Ewha Archives]

Dr. Kim visited and spoke in Los Angeles, San Francisco, Chicago, Detroit, New York, Philadelphia, Baltimore, Washington, DC,

Atlanta, and San Diego. In spite of her colon cancer operation shortly before in February 1989, she was laying down her life for her commitment and love for Ewha and friends of Ewha. Foundation Board member Joseph Yi commented in the Summer 1989 issue of the Foundation's *Ewha News* that Dr. Kim's speaking tour taught him a new definition of *COMMITMENT*. Her speaking tour heartened the alumnae and, in response to her personal appeals, many friends and alumnae pledged over $300,000. Dr. Kim's tour resulted in forming the local alumnae chapters in Houston and San Diego. In addition to the tour, she paid visits to Dr. Betty Mitchell at her home in Tucson, Arizona, and to Dr. Mamie Lee Finger at her home. These two friends were special to Dr. Helen Kim and for Ewha because of their dedication for establishing the International Foundation and their efforts that resulted in the building of the Centennial Library. Dr. Kim returned home after the very successful and strenuous speaking tour.

Dr. Ogkill Kim graduated from Ewha College in 1943, attended Ohio Wesleyan University in 1949-1952, and Temple University in 1957 for graduate work. She received an honorary doctorate from Ewha Womans University in 1961. She succeeded Dr. Helen Kim as Ewha's president in 1961. She served as the President for 18 years from 1961 to 1979. Subsequently, she served as the Chair of the Board of Trustees of Ewha Womans University from 1979 to 1990. She passed away on August 25, 1990.

"Putting Our Feet Forward on Education": 1989-1995

The leadership of Julia K. Wilke as President of the Foundation from 1989 to 1995 marked the expansion of Foundation constituents. She and her husband, Bishop Richard Wilke, were inspired by their visit to Ewha Womans University. She and President Chung Ii-sook shared ideas and gained insights into the distinguished university.

In the Winter 1989 issue of the Foundation's *Ewha News*, Mrs. Wilke reported on her trip to Korea and challenged the alumnae and friends of Ewha to give to the newly created Helen Kim Lectureship Endowment. Mrs. Wilke commented on their visit to Ewha, "I have heard it said that we must put 'feet on our prayers' – pray and then follow the Lord's guidance and do something. I feel Ewha is 'putting feet on education.'" She then wrote:

Would you help us to "put feet on education." President Ii Sook Chung has asked us to raise $100,000 to endow a lectureship for visiting scholars. These outstanding scholars from all over the world would greatly enhance the scope of knowledge made available to the students. It is to be called the Helen Kim Endowed Lectureship, remembering Helen Kim not only for her presidency at Ewha but also her world vision.[43]

Mrs. Wilke felt strongly that we are blessed in order that we might become a blessing. And through us, by God's grace, help others to bless themselves. Her prayer for Ewha was "to continue to be a blessing in order that the abundant life might come to the people of Korea – and through them and us – to the people of the whole world." Her reflections demonstrated her personal commitment to strengthening the *River of Faith* that was serving Ewha so well. Additionally, her comments offered a spiritual perspective to the new role Ewha President Chung Ii-sook had recently announced, which was advancing Ewha from being the receiving university to a giving university.

5th President, IFEWU, Mrs. Julia K. Wilke
[International Foundation Archives]

The Foundation under the faithful leadership of Mrs. Wilke benefited in many

Ewha's Maple Leaf Community Service Center [Ewha Archives]

ways, including an expansion in the numbers of Ewha alumnae participating in the Foundation's activities. Representatives of the local Ewha alumnae associations were invited to join the Annual meetings. The representatives were asked to report and share information on the activities of the local chapters, including those related to fundraising. The participation of the local chapter representatives was warmly welcomed, although voting on Foundation matters was reserved for Board members.

The partnership with Canada was highly commended since during the previous two decades Canadians had contributed via the International Foundation more than $500,000 to Ewha through several organizations. Examples of their contributions are as follows: The Canadian Board of the Christian Children's Fund ($20,000, $40,000), The United Church of Canada ($3,000, $3,000, $3,100, $3,000, $2,880, $2,972, $3,100, $2,832), the Canadian International Development Agency ($100,000, $40,000), Ewha Alumnae Canada Chapter ($1,500, $10,000 and the

Mr. Frank J. Whilsmith [International Foundation Archives]

start-up of the Toronto Ewha Alumnae Endowment for $100,000), and contributions for the Ewha Speech and Hearing Center ($1,300 sent directly to Ewha by the Frank Whilsmith Foundation).

Mr. Frank J. Whilsmith, a Canadian, was an outstanding Board member dedicated to the development of the Foundation as an international and ecumenical organization. Mr. Whilsmith was a Board member for about two decades from 1974 onward. He served on the Committee on Promotion and Public Relations for the period 1975-1985. During the same years he was Chairman of the Presbyterian Church in Canada Administrative Council. He had owned his own advertising company in Toronto before founding the Christian Children's Fund of Canada which he served as Chairman and President of the Board for many years.

Mr. Whilsmith was especially interested in the Ewha Community Service Center and assisted the Center through the Children's Fund and a Canadian Government agency. To honor the Canadian contributions, the Center changed its name to the Maple Leaf Community Service Center. Mr. Whilsmith established the Whilsmith Scholarship Fund in 1990 and also supported many other projects in Korea. In total, Mr. Whilsmith directed or contributed nearly $1,000,000 to Ewha.

In Celebration of the Foundation's First Twenty Years: 1989

In September 1989, on the occasion of the 20th year of the International Foundation, a summation was made of financial accomplishments. The growing investments, contributions, and investment income set a record in 1989 with a total market value of over $2,000,000. Over the 20 years of its existence, the Foundation remitted to Ewha $3,000,000. During the year 1989, the Foundation sent $130,407 to Ewha. A total of $58,877 was spent that same year for library books and other purchases that were shipped to Ewha Womans University.

Looking back on the International Foundation's first 20 years, it was amply evident that a fully functional, structurally sound, and sustainable organization with a well-defined mission had evolved. With it came an extremely strong sense of mutual dedication and rapport among the participating friends of Ewha, the Ewha University leadership, Ewha alumnae, and members of the families of Ewha alumnae. The common glue bonding the group was the Christian-based mission to educate women in Korea.

Dr. Mamie Lee Finger, recognized for her fundraising skills during her Foundation presidency, continued to apply her expertise as the chair of the Special Gifts Committee. She proposed the establishment of the Helen Kim Endowment Fund (later to become the Helen Kim International Lectureship) in honor of Helen Kim as a faithful visionary, a proponent of internationalism, and as the founder of the International Foundation. She contributed $1,000 as the first person to start the Fund towards its $100,000 goal in 1989. Many Board members also followed with support. In response to a suggestion by Ewha President Chung Ii-sook and conveyed by Foundation President Wilke, the fund was dedicated to inviting distinguished lecturers to Ewha.

In her quest for funding sources, Dr. Finger approached the Luce

Foundation. Dr. James Laney, a former International Foundation Board member, had recently been appointed a trustee of the Luce Foundation. The Rev. Dr. Laney had served as a missionary to Korea where he taught at Yonsei University. He served as president of Emory University for 16 years, was formerly the ambassador of the U.S. to Korea, and was a personal friend of the Fingers and Dr. Helen Kim. Dr. Finger wrote a proposal to the Luce Foundation for a grant of $25,000 for the Helen Kim International Lectureship, which would bring the fund to its goal of $100,000. The proposal was funded. The first lecture supported by the Endowment was given by Dr. James Laney, who was accompanied by his wife, as part of the celebration of the 20th Anniversary of the International Foundation.

Dedication at its Finest

In practically every organization there are individuals who become involved fortuitously, but because of their unique skills, dedication, and steady perseverance they prove crucial to the organization's success. Mr. Moon Pyo Hong was such a person for the International Foundation. Mr. Hong first served as a trusted staff member and confidante for Dr. Helen Kim as she labored to create the Foundation. He then functioned as the Foundation's associate director and then executive director.

Foundation Executive Director
Mr. Moon Pyo Hong
[International Foundation Archives]

Dr. Helen Kim had come to the U.S. in 1967 to establish the North American component of the Ewha Decade Development Program. She was searching for competent staff to assist in its administration. She asked Mr. Oh Jae Kyung, Secretary of the Information Ministry in Korea, if he could make any suggestions. He recommended a young man, Mr. Moon Pyo Hong, who he knew was living in the Washington, DC area. Mr. Hong had worked in the Information Ministry in Korea and later as an Information Attaché in the Korean Embassy in Washington.

Mr. Hong had been in the U.S. since 1963. He agreed to work for Dr. Helen Kim and planned to assist her for a few years as she established what was to become the International Foundation. He helped Dr. Kim by doing whatever tasks needed to be done. He also provided transportation for Dr. Kim in his 1967 Plymouth Fury automobile as she otherwise had only public transportation available to her. In order to save the expenses of air travel, Mr. Hong drove Dr. Kim on long fundraising trips to Lake Junaluska, Boston, South Bend, Hartford, New Haven, Chicago, Detroit, and Toronto, Canada. Mr. Hong fondly recalled the long periods of driving while Dr. Kim punctuated the hours of travel by singing beautiful hymns, as well as popular songs such as the Korean *A Man in a Yellow Shirt*. "She depended on me to travel by the car in order to save the travel expenses and she stayed at YMCA hotels as they were inexpensive. She paid my wage from her own pocket."

Upon the creation of the International Foundation, Mr. Hong became a staff member. He was the Associate Director from 1970 to October 1971 and the Executive Secretary from 1971 to 1993. His work included all facets of office operation while conducting Foundation programs and implementing new initiatives as directed by the president and executive committee. He was involved in banking and disbursement matters, prepared financial reports, managed the preparation and mailing of the Foundation *Ewha News* newsletter, prepared and dealt with the details of fundraising, prepared for and coordinated annual meetings, communicated with Board members, and interacted with Ewha alumnae and friends of Ewha. He was heavily involved for years in the promotion and processing of Ewha International Summer School applications. He seldom had secretarial assistance.

Shortly after its creation, the Foundation's office was located in the

United Board for Christian Higher Education in Asia in the Interchurch Center, in Manhattan, New York, This enabled Mr. Hong to have access to other non-profit Christian charity organizations such as International Medical Assistance (IMA). He secured medical equipment from IMA that was sent to the hospital run by Ewha Womans University Medical College.

In 1989, the Foundation Board presented Mr. Hong a plaque of appreciation and a gift for his dedication and excellent work. In 1993, he was awarded a plaque of appreciation presented by President Yoon Hoo-jung of Ewha Womans University in recognition of the assistance he gave for many years processing applications of prospective students for the Ewha International Summer School. Mr. Hong retired in 1993 from the Foundation, which was immensely grateful for his decades of faithful service. Although his involvement had started by happenstance because of Dr. Helen Kim's need for assistance as she worked to create the Foundation, he too became a part of the Ewha *River of Faith*.

Mrs. Jaeyonne Kim succeeded Mr. Hong as the Foundation's Executive Director in December 1993. Her tenure at the Foundation office saw the 1995 introduction of new technology to better manage rapidly expanding data bases, documentation, and communications. In 1997, Mrs. Miran Kim assumed the role of the Executive Director for three years. In 2000, Mrs. Ji-yei Song Park became the Executive Director.

Growing Alumnae Participation Brings Change: 1990 and Beyond

By 1990, stirrings surfaced among local Ewha alumnae associations to seek greater definition of their organizational relationships with the International Foundation and Ewha. Similar thoughts had also been expressed by Board members in previous years of the relationship between the Foundation and alumnae. For example, in the minutes of the 19th Annual Meeting held in November 1988, describing the discussion of the Committee on Promotion and Public Relations' report, Board Member "Mr. Whilsmith expressed concern that the committee is not relating as well as it might with alumnae groups. The committee therefore expressed its desire to have Ewha alumnae appointed as members of the committee." Presumably, it was referring to the addition of Ewha alumnae active in local chapters who were not Board members.

Because the origins of most of the local chapters were due to activities related to the Foundation, especially for fundraising for Ewha channeled through the Foundation, a strong affinity evolved and a sense of partnership had emerged. From the perspective of members of the Foundation Board, enthusiastic support for ties between the Foundation and local chapters were expressed by individuals such as Dr. Betty Mitchell, Dr. Mimie Lee Finger, Mrs. Julia Wilke, Dr. Kilchai Yim, Dr. Hai Won Chang, Mr. Joseph Yi, and Dr. Soon Ja Choi. To address the issue, representatives of 13 local Ewha Alumnae Chapters met and discussed how local chapters might best be aligned with the Foundation and given voice within the organizational structure of the Foundation. The consensus was to have representatives of the local chapters join the Foundation Board as Adjunct Board Members.

Dr. Hai Won Chang, Chair of the Foundation's Committee on Nominations, played a leading role as the By-Laws Committee reviewed the proposal to create adjunct Board memberships. The review was conducted in consultation with Dr. Soon Ja Choi. Dr. Choi acted as liaison with the group of local Ewha Alumnae Chapter representatives proposing change.

The By-Laws Committee proposed the following motion that was considered at the 1990 Annual Board Meeting:

> *The adjunct members of the Foundation shall be selected from those who serve as Presidents of the Local Alumnae Associations of Ewha*

Womans University in the United States and Canada. They or their representatives shall be invited to attend the annual meeting and any special meetings of the Foundation as non-voting members. They may engage in any deliberations of the Board, make recommendations to the Board on any subject, and, in coordination with the Board, carry out Board decisions relating to the Local Alumnae Associations they represent.[44]

The motion of the modification of the By-Laws regarding Adjunct Board Membership was carried unanimously.

The first two decades of the Foundation's existence had seen remarkably little change in the Foundation Board membership. In its early years, the Board consisted primarily of American-born members, mostly friends of Dr. Helen Kim. Among the Korean Americans who were invited by Dr. Kim to be among the earliest Board members were Dr. Kilchai Yim, Dr. Hai Won Chang, Dr. Bumsun Lee, Mrs. Bessie Kim, Mr. P. William Lee, Mr. Sae Sun Kim, Rev. Henry Oh, And Dr. Myung Soon Oh. These and other Korean-American Board members, as evidenced by the minutes of Annual Meetings, distinguished themselves with decades of service to the Foundation in leadership roles. The ethnic composition of the Board had remained much the same because of little turnover. Most were past friends or acquaintances of Helen Kim and had intense commitments to assist their beloved Ewha.

In a personal interview, Dr. Hai Won Chang, Chair of the Committee on Nominations from 1980 to 2002, indicated the Board was initially maintained at 30 members By the mid-1990s, it was raised to the maximum of 35 as allowed by Article IV of the Foundation's Constitution. In 2006, Article IV was revised to raise the Board membership to not more than 39 persons. The backgrounds of potential Board members were carefully reviewed in terms of academic background, ethnic background, and potential financial support for the Foundation. The resumes of the

Board candidates were carefully reviewed by the Committee.

The key element of a recommendation is the balance and the spirit the potential Board member demonstrates for Ewha. Most of the original Board members were Dr. Helen Kim's friends or persons connected to those friends. When they left due to retirement, advanced age, or death, new members replacing the old were selected as appropriate to bring ethnic balance to the Board. The goal was to have on the Board equal numbers of indigenous North Americans (Americans and Canadians) and Korean Americans, including Ewha graduates and their relatives. In summation, the policy of the Committee on Nominations was to balance countries of origin, geographic regions in North America, gender, and age while reviewing the potential for providing the Foundation with expertise and potential to generate resources for the ultimate benefit of Ewha Womans University.

By 1993, of the 30 Board members, 14 were natives of North America, 13 were Ewha alumnae and three were family members of Ewha graduates. The Adjunct Board Memberships that had been created with the intention of fostering closer connections between local alumnae and the Foundation grew for several years, but faded away due to the lack of nominations from the field.

Dr. Hai Won Chang
[International Foundation Archives]

Dr. Hai Won Chang served the Foundation since its beginning, and she played an indispensable role in shaping the Foundation through her steady service in a number of roles. Perhaps her most significant role was her administration of the Foundation's nomination process. She and her husband, Dr. Soon Man Rhim, were among the founding members of the Ewha Development Committee of New York in 1966. Dr. Chang was an International Foundation

Board member from its beginning until 2003.

After 2003, she continued serving the Foundation as an Honorary Member and the Chair of the Advisory Council.

Dr. Chang graduated from Ewha University in 1950 as a Pharmacy major. She came to the U.S. in 1953, completed a Master's degree in Chemistry from Wellesley College, and was awarded a Ph.D. in Chemistry from Columbia University in 1961. She remained at Columbia University as a postdoctoral research and faculty member until her retirement in 1991. She has been an active member of Ewha Womans University Alumnae Association of New York since its founding in 1964.

Dr. Chang contributed financially to the Foundation through scholarship funds and partaking in Ewha Womans University's various fund-raising requests, such as the building funds for the Centennial Memorial Library, Mokdong Hospital, new College of Pharmacy building, and the Twenty-First Century Development Fund. At the time of her retirement from Columbia University in 1991, the entire laboratory equipment and lab ware from her Neurochemistry research laboratory were donated to Ewha when she returned to Ewha as a visiting professor. The value of the equipment at the time was about $150,000.

She was given an appreciation plaque by the International Foundation at its 22nd Annual Meeting and was the honored recipient of a *Distinguished Ewhaian* Award by Ewha Womans University in May 2002.

The early years of the 1990s marked a period of dramatic increase in the participation of Ewha alumnae in North America in local chapters that deepened feelings of sisterhood while accelerating fundraising activities as expressions of their love for Ewha. The International Foundation could take pride in its role as a nexus strengthening the already strong bonds between the growing numbers of Ewha alumnae in North America with their beloved Ewha.

Through Dr. Betty Mitchell's strong leadership in the first decade of the Foundation and the commitment of Dr. Okgill Kim in using her final life's energy to campaign for local alumnae chapter development and fundraising, the International Foundation grew into a viable instrument dedicated to acquiring resources for Ewha. Dr. Mamie Lee Finger's vitality, fortitude, and vision for fundraising as she championed partnerships with Ewha alumnae helped grow the Foundation further. Throughout the Foundation's existence, but accelerating in the 1990s, the Ewha alumnae were making their presence known. Many alumnae families in North America were maturing with successful professional careers established or behind them, enabling them to share their good fortune with others, including current and future students at Ewha. The Foundation nurtured these philanthropic instincts through greater involvement with alumnae through the local chapters and mailings. The *Ewha News*, now the *Ewha Foundation News*, was conceived as part of the ongoing effort to inform alumnae and friends of Ewha of Foundation progress, news from Ewha regarding support received through the Foundation, alumnae chapter's activities, and fundraising results. Since 1995 the newsletter has typically been bilingual.

Local Ewha Alumnae Chapters began participating in Board meetings in 1989, and made presentations to the Board. In 1990, under the heading of Alumnae Chapter News, the New York, Chicago, Detroit, Lehigh Valley, Southern California and Washington, DC Chapters reported on their fundraising activities. The 1991 Newsletter introduced the Presidents of 18 chapters.

In 1992, the Foundation Board created the Alumnae Relations Committee (ARC) to meet the repeatedly expressed desire to be more closely tied to the local alumnae chapters. The purpose was to insure that Board members will be able to take part in meetings of alumnae representatives when they coincide with Board committee meetings.

Mrs. Shirley Jeffery, Chair of the Committee on Promotion and Public Relations, presided at the first meeting of the ARC with six members of the Board and eight alumnae representing five chapters attending.

Board member Dr. Soon Ja Choi became the ARC chair. The ARC immediately began to plan ways to contact potential new members in the then existing 20 local chapters. The committee decided to include news columns of alumnae chapters in *Ewha News*. For the fundraising, May Day letters would be sent out to the alumnae.

The number of representatives from local chapters attending ARC meetings grew quickly in the early 1990s. By 1994, the ARC meeting was attended by 32 representatives from 12 local chapters. The Annual Meeting the following year had 35 alumnae attending. They reported on their chapter activities.

Alumnae, especially with the creation of local alumnae chapters, were busy raising funds on their own initiatives. In March 1989, Ewha Womans University and its teaching Hospital announced a drive to raise $4 million targeted towards alumnae to help fund the $50 million new hospital complex planned for Mokdong in Seoul. This was in addition to the Professor Exchange Program, Research Fund, Helen Kim Memorial Lectureship Fund, and individual alumnae chapter scholarship endowments, to which Ewha was being supported via their contributions.

There are numerous examples of local chapter fundraising. In 1989, the Detroit Chapter had its annual dinner on November 13, 1989 with 85 alumnae pledging $3,400 towards the new hospital and the Helen Kim Lectureship Fund. The Lehigh Valley Chapter of Pennsylvania had a fundraising dinner with 35 alumnae attending. The dinner raised $2,500. The Southern California Chapter held its annual dinner in December 1989 attended by 200, and raised over $15,000 for Mokdong Hospital and $3,000 toward the Helen Kim Memorial Lectureship Fund.

The New York Chapter, at its 1989 annual dinner attended by 180 alumnae, raised $6,000 for the New York Alumnae Scholarship Endowment Fund which, from 1982 to 1989, totaled $100,000 for the Ewha Faculty Continuing Education Scholarship Fund. The Chapter also raised $3,500 for the Helen Kim Memorial Lectureship. By 1994, the NY

Alumnae Scholarship Fund had amassed a total of $150,000. The New York fundraising efforts were spearheaded by Dr. Hyang Won Lee.

Dr. Hyang Won Lee was a member of the first graduating class of the Ewha College of Medicine in 1951. She came to the U.S. for medical training in 1953 through an internship in Obstetrics/Gynecology at the Margaret Hague Maternity Hospital and a residency at Unity Hospital as well as at the Jamaica Hospital Medical Center. In 1959, Dr. Lee accepted a Jamaica Hospital pathology residency. She worked for 43 years in the hospital's Pathology Department, during which she became Chairperson of the Department in 1997. She taught residents in the Obstetrics/Gynecology residency program from 1985 to 2000. She was also a clinical assistant professor of pathology at State University of New York Downstate Medical Center from 1981 to 1993.

She was an advisor and Chair of the Board of Trustees of the Ewha Womans University Alumnae Association for Greater New York. She had been a member of Ewha Decade Development Committee in 1969. Dr. Hyang Won Lee and her husband Dr. Bumsun Lee, long-time Treasurer of the Foundation, have been devoted supporters of the International Foundation since its inception.

In 2003, Dr. Hyang Won Lee was a recipient of the *Distinguished Ewhaian* Award at Ewha Womans University's 117th Founder's Day Ceremony.

Other examples of fundraising include the Washington, DC Chapter's Scholarship Endowment Fund established in 1992 that had raised $27,000 by 1994. Part of the successful fundraising was due to the use of a creative version of the Korean "KEH" that had been devised by the Houston Alumnae Chapter in 1992. "KEH" is a traditional Korean form of micro-financing mostly used by women to acquire funds for business or family use. The former Houston Alumnae President, Mrs. Jung Hee Kong Choi, informed others of Houston's fundraising innovation. The Washington "KEH" club, first with 20 alumnae participants and then with 30, was organized by Mrs. Yaun Dahm Yoo Han. Over two years, the Washington, DC Chapter's use of the "KEH" club approach raised $10,000 for its Scholarship Endowment Fund. Mrs. Han became a Foundation Board Member in 1993.

In 1997, the Washington, DC Alumnae Chapter led by alumna Dr. Chang Hyun Shin Geer sponsored a music concert by the Seoul Chamber Orchestra directed by Ewha Professor Kim Youngun. The concert, performed in the George Washington University Lisner Auditorium, raised $10,000 for the Washington, DC Scholarship Endowment Fund.

The San Francisco Alumnae Chapter carried out fundraising activities during 1993-1994 which netted $5,000.

Ewha alumnae living in the Houston area had been greatly inspired by Dr. Okgill Kim's visit in 1989. The Houston Alumnae Chapter was formed that year. During a memorial service they held for Dr. Kim in 1990, the members contributed $43,000 for a scholarship endowment.

On May 24, 1991, the Chicago Alumnae Chapter sponsored a concert by violinist Eunice Lee at Ewha Womans University in Seoul and raised $80,000 for the Ewha's Mokdong Hospital Building Fund. The concert was arranged mainly by Mr. and Mrs. Joseph (Soong Ok) Yi, who escorted Ms. Lee during the trip. The grandmother of the highly regarded violinist Eunice Lee was an Ewha graduate. On August 1, 1992, Eunice Lee presented a concert also arranged by the Yi's on the Northwestern University campus sponsored by the International Foundation and hosted by the Chicago Alumnae Chapter. It netted almost $20,000 for Ewha's benefit.

Marking the 25th Anniversary of the Foundation: 1995

Mrs. Julia K. Wilke joyfully celebrated the 25th Anniversary of the International Foundation at its Annual Meeting held in New York on November 4, 1994. Present were the President of Ewha Womans University,

Dr. Yoon Hoo-jung, and International Foundation charter members, Mrs. Eunice Beene, Dr. Kilchai K. Yim, Dr. Hai Won Chang, and Dr. Bumsun Lee. Also present were past Foundation Presidents Betty Mitchell, Mamie Lee Finger, and Susan Ruby Lamb, and 22 Board members. President Yoon gave a special speech pointing out Ewha accomplishments leading toward to the 21st century. The Banquet was prepared under the leadership of Mrs. Byoung Dai Lim Hahm, who was the president of the New York local chapter.

By the early 1990s, ample evidence was emerging of the accomplishments of Ewha as it was moving towards a world-recognized institution of higher education. Noteworthy Ewha achievements during 1993-1994, for example, included breaking the myth about women's scientific abilities, proved by the opening of Mokdong Hospital, the opening of four departments in the new College of Engineering, a new annex building with laboratory and research facilities for the College of Pharmacy, and the launching of an up-to-date computer network called Ewha-net integrating educational, research, and administrative functions. Also lauded was the recognition that the Ewha Basic Science Research Institute had been designated as one of the best science institutes in Korea, and the good news that Ewha's Physics and Chemistry Departments were graded "excellent" by the Ministry of Education and the Korean Council of University Education.

Mrs. Carol Murdoch, Foundation Secretary, described in the Winter 1995 issue of *Ewha News* the illuminating vision of Ewha's President Yoon Hoo-jung who had reported to the International Foundation at its 25th Annual Meeting in November 1994.

President Yoon started her report by saying, "I feel great pride and deep responsibility as I report on the remarkable achievements and changes Ewha has made over the past year to become the world's best institute for higher learning for women, and the painstaking efforts Ewha has made to prepare for the 21st century."

In the same Winter 1995 issue of *Ewha News*, from excerpts taken directly from the Ewha President's Address at the International Foundation's Silver Anniversary Banquet, Dr. Yoon Hoo-jung said:

> *As you are keenly aware, national, racial and language barriers are rapidly collapsing throughout the world, making peoples of different origins live together in one global village, waging a non-violet war of unlimited competition. Universities are no exception to such a trend. ... The 21st century holds the promise of a new world order, a higher quality of life and the internationalization of women. Because society will be more pluralistic and decentralized than ever before, women will have boundless chances for self-realization and leadership. While the first 108 years saw Ewha expanding women's access to education, the second 108 years will see Ewha bringing up professional women who will play a substantial role not only in Korean society but also in the world. Ewha is thus reminded of the call it heard at the time of its birth.*[45]

President Yoon then looked forward, indicating that priorities for the future included further development of science education, internationalization, systematic utilization of information, and welfare enhancement. She then proceeded to vision plans for Ewha's 21st century. She spoke of ways Ewha was planning to finance the realization of its priorities. She described Ewha's 21st Century Development Program that had been created with a goal of raising $125 million, of which in the first four months of its creation had received donations of about $30 million.

In line with the goals of Ewha to generate support for Ewha's continued development, the International Foundation and its members were enthusiastic supporters and contributors. Physicians, such as Dr. Kilchai Yim, Vice President of the Foundation, and Dr. Soon Ja Choi, Chair of the Alumnae Relations Committee, had spearheaded fundraising for the

Mokdong Hospital, Ewha's teaching hospital. Ewha alumnae trained in medicine at Ewha joined the campaign with zealous love for progress of their alma master's medical school.

Ewha's 10th President Yoon Hoo-jung [Ewha Archives]

As was happening almost everywhere, the introduction of personal computers and the Internet into the workplace in the early and mid-1990s enabled the International Foundation's office operation to be upgraded by lessening tedious manual work while greatly facilitating processes for fundraising, communications, and bookkeeping. This was especially significant for the one-person Foundation office operation. The modernization was given special impetus in 1994 as Mrs. Jaeyonne Kim, replacing Mr. Moon Pyo Hong as the Executive Director, introduced electronic processing and storage of documents and data. The change was fortuitous because of the growth and increasing complexity of the Foundation's administration.

Mokdong Hospital Building: "Love and Devotion in Ewha Consciousness"

One of Ewha's 21st Century Development Program goals was to build the Mokdong Hospital. The Foundation's assistance for the building of the Ewha University Mokdong Hospital in Seoul was a significant achievement built on 25 years of dedication. Included in the assistance was the demonstration of compassion for the healing process exhibited through the contribution of building funds for the hospital's chapel. Dr. Kilchai Yim contributed $50,000 towards the chapel construction in 1994. The total contribution from the Board, alumnae, and friends of Ewha for Mokdong Hospital over a five-year period was $520,000. On the opening day of the hospital, Dr. Chung Ii-sook, Chair of the University's Board of Trustees, said:

> *... the basis of the Ewha consciousness is love and devotion. We think of each patient as a loved one, and it is a role to be devoted to those in pain. With this fundamental philosophy in mind, we found it our duty to embark in the creation of this new hospital.*[46]

There are numerous examples that can be given of the strong love and devotion Ewha Medical School graduates showed through their contributions to the building of Mokdong Hospital. Dr. Sook Hie Han Yu, a 1959 graduate of the Ewha University Medical School, gave a sculpture created by Sanford Werfel, entitled *The Tree of Life*, placed in the foyer of the Mokdong Hospital. In her own words, Dr. Yu said:

> *The Lord God planted all sorts of beautiful trees there in the Garden [of Eden], trees producing the choicest of Fruit. At the center of the*

Ewha Womans University Medical Center (Mokdong Hospital) [Ewha Archives]

garden, He placed the Tree of Life and the Tree of Conscience ... [*Genesis 2:9*]

Mokdong Hospital's *The Tree of Life*, donated by Dr. Sook Hie Han Yu [Ewha Archives]

No person who passes through Ewha's gate is immortal, but the knowledge that Ewha University embodies is immortal ... . The Tree of Life sculpture that hangs in the hospital foyer is an appropriate symbol of the commitment to quality teaching and health care at Ewha University Hospital ... .[47]

Dr. Sook Hie Han Yu served as the President of Philadelphia Ewha Alumnae Association in 1993 and served as a Foundation Board Member from 1993 to 1997.

Part 7

Service and Progress

Shaping International Exchange Programs

The vitality of the Foundation can be attributed to the partnering across national boundaries very much in alignment with the spirit of internationalism on which Ewha has been based since its beginning. At the April 15, 1970 Inaugural Meeting of the International Foundation, Mrs. E. L. Hillman had strongly conveyed the relationship among Ewha, the U.S., and Canada, and the enrichment and benefits derived by all partners of the relationship.[48]

The Foundation has promoted internationalism in its composition, associations, and fundraising. It has encouraged and supported a wide variety of University efforts to provide advanced study and research opportunities abroad for Ewha faculty members, to bring international scholars to the Ewha campus, to bring students from around the world to Ewha's campus, and to host international conferences such as those focusing on women's studies.

The Foundation facilitated two major channels acting as a clearing

Ewha International Summer School Students

house of information to North American students exploring study opportunities at Ewha and assistance for Ewha faculty development in the U.S. through Seabury Foundation grants and a New York Alumnae Association grant.

The Foundation continued its management of the application process in the U.S. for the International Summer School in Asian Studies program at Ewha University that was started in 1971. It evolved into a program for coed university students.

Scholarships were established through the Foundation to encourage U.S. students to have summer learning experiences at Ewha. Notably, the Gloria Hahn Scholarship was established by Dr. Richard S. Hahn and his friends in memory of his wife, Gloria Hahn (Kim Ronyoung) in 1989. The endowment is used to encourage students of the U.S. to study Asian culture studies in Ewha Summer Institute in Seoul, Korea.

Although not directly funded through the International Foundation, Board member Mrs. Eunice Beene arranged a unique program at Lon

Morris College, located in Jacksonville, Texas, to send two of its students to the Ewha Summer Institute in 1988. The program, supported by income from an endowment she had established in memory of her parents, continued for years.

Moving into the New Millennium: 1996-2000

In 1996, the Foundation welcomed a new President, Mrs. Susanne Lamb Stevens. She was the daughter of Susan Ruby Lamb, the third President of the Foundation. She had become a Board member in 1987 and served on the Committee on Finance. She served as President from 1996 to 1999. She was the Vice President of Instruction at Skyline College near San Francisco, California.

6th President, IFEWU,
Mrs. Susanne L. Stevens
[International Foundation Archives]

In 1996, the Foundation welcomed the new Ewha University President, Dr. Chang Sang. President Chang addressed the Foundation Board at its Annual Meeting. As recorded in the Meeting's minutes, she proclaimed a new vision for Ewha as it approached the 21st century:

I have had an awesome awareness that this time is a turning point for Ewha. ... The distinguishing marks of this time are that it is both the age of globalization and the information age. ... In the 21st century, it is the globalization of Ewha. The Ewha of the 21st century is not simply Korea's Ewha. It must be the world's Ewha. ... Dr. Helen Kim started this Ewha International Foundation in the late 1960s, ever since that time the Foundation has been sowing the seeds of globalization for Ewha. I know of no other university in Korea which could even have thought of having such an overseas connection, so Ewha has been truly blessed.[49]

Ewha's 11th President Chang Sang [Ewha Archives]

During President Chang Sang's tenure, this new task of Ewha, globalization, became known as Ewha's *Vision 21*.

The Foundation, by 1996, consisted of 32 Board members, 27 adjunct Board members, and 11 honorary Board members. The Foundation had become a large family of 71 including the Executive Director. During this year, Ms. Miran Kim became the new Executive Director of the Foundation.

By 1996, a significant change in fundraising had evolved through greater participation and giving by Ewha alumna and friends. The leadership of Foundation President Susanne L. Stevens, with the dynamic dedication of Dr. Soon Ja Choi, Chair of the Alumnae Relations Committee, and aided by the fervent commitment of alumna throughout the U.S. and Canada, produced dramatic results. Evidence of the change in fundraising was shown by the increase in individual endowments. There were three established endowments in 1971, and by 1997 there were 58.

The Alumnae Relations Committee (ARC) created four Sub-Committees; the Recruiting Committee, the Publication Committee, the Fundraising Committee, and Medical School Committee. The Recruiting Committee was to recruit alumna to participate in the annual meeting of the Ewha Alumnae Association of North America each year. The Co-chairs were Mrs. In Hee Ryu Kim and Mrs. Il Sun Chang. The Publication Committee was to publish the newsletter of the Alumnae Association. The Co-Chairs were Mrs. Hae Soon Kim and Mrs. Young Ju Chun. The Fundraising Committee was to establish the Ewha International

Alumnae Endowment Fund. The ARC Fundraising Committee was led by Co-chairs Mrs. Jai Kang Chu Song and Dr. Hwain Chang Lee. The International Alumnae Endowment Fund set the goal of raising $100 per alumna from 1,000 alumnae. The Medical School Committee was chaired by two graduates of the Medical College, Dr. Yong Ok Cho and Dr. Ok Hee Won. The Medical School Committee established the Medical Research Endowment Fund for Ewha.

Finance Investments: 1971-2009

The Foundation's Committee on Finance has three responsibilities; supervision of investments and securities, preparation of an annual administrative budget, and disbursements to Ewha. Its Investment Subcommittee has the responsibilities of monitoring investments held by the Foundation and changing them as market conditions change, as well as reporting investment performance to the Finance Committee and to the Board. The Foundation treasurer serves in an oversight capacity.

Mrs. Kathryne B. Sears served as the first chairperson of the Committee on Finance, and was a member of the Investment Sub-committee.

Dr. Bumsun Lee was Associate Treasurer for the Foundation in 1971 and 1972. Starting in 1972, he served as the Treasurer of the Foundation until 2009. He received his MBA and Ph.D. in Accounting and Finance from New York University and his Certified Public Accountant License from the State of New York. He was a professor of accounting at Long Island University, New York. His expertise made him the ideal Foundation Treasurer.

Dr. Bumsun Lee
[International Foundation Archives]

Dr. Bumsun Lee contributed to the

Mr. Mark Gaston
[International Foundation Archives]

Foundation as Treasurer for almost forty years. He expressed that even though he had been teaching as a university professor and was a CPA, he most enjoyed his work with the Foundation because of its help for Ewha. He said he served the Foundation because of his love for his wife and his way of repaying his debt to Ewha for his wife, Dr. Hyang Won Lee.

Dr. Bumsun Lee carefully presented and filed an annual financial report every year for 40 years since the beginning of the Foundation. In recognition of his service, he was awarded an Appreciation Plaque by the Foundation at its 17th Annual Meeting in 1986. Also, Dr. Lee was the recipient of the honorary degree of Doctor of Liberal Arts in 1988 at Ewha Womans University graduation ceremony in Seoul, Korea.

The portfolio of the funds had been managed by the Irving Trust Company since the existence of the Ewha Cooperating Board of the North America. Mr. Mark Gaston, as a vice president of Irving Trust, managed the Foundation account and attended Foundation meetings. In 1993, Mr. Gaston became a Board member. Mr. Gaston served as a member of the Committee on Finance as Co-chair and Chair of the Investment Sub-committee.

Mr. Mark Gaston is the President of Gaston Capital Management, Inc., a manager of investment accounts in the U.S. and an advisor to investors abroad. He is a Chartered Financial Analyst and has a bachelor's degree from Johns Hopkins University and an MBA from Drexel University.

In 1993, the Irving Trust joined with the Bank of New York in managing the Foundation's investment portfolio. During that same year, Dr. Gerald O'Mara, Chair of the Finance Committee, proposed the modification of procedures for management and oversight. After almost 25 years, the Foundation had become a much larger organization facing new challenges. The proposal called for establishing an Operations Committee made up of four Board members with the President and Chair of the Finance Committee serving *ex officio*. Approval, in writing, would be required of at least one member for any transaction involving a significant amount of money. Such a committee would provide substantial support for the executive director. It was unanimously approved and the committee recommended that four Board members living in the New York area become the Board's Operational Committee. Dr. Kilchai Yim, Dr. Bumsun Lee, Dr. Hai Won Chang, and Dr. Michael Hahm were members of the first committee, with Dr. Yim serving as Chair.

The guidelines for the Operations Committee were delineated and the Board unanimously approved them: "The Foundation should not borrow money to finance its investment objectives. The Foundation should never lend to other organizations or individuals. That is, the Foundation should not behave as either a banker or an arbitrageur."

In the following year (1994), the Finance Committee discussed the performance of the Foundation's investment manager, the Bank of New York, in comparison with that of other firms. After the considerable reviews and discussion, the Foundation launched an innovative investment method. The Foundation would discontinue the management of the investment of the Foundation under the Bank of New York in order to achieve a diversified portfolio of no-load mutual funds composed of equities, bonds and money market funds in proportions that would maximize returns while minimizing risk. This approach would yield higher overall returns and lower management costs.

The Board unanimously approved that the Foundation change its method of investment management. The new investment method was implemented by the Investment Sub-committee composed of Dr. O'Mara, Dr. Bumsun Lee, Dr. Kilchai Yim, and Mr. Mark Gaston, with Dr. Yim and Mr. Gaston as co-chairs. Because of his expertise and willingness to serve, Mr. Gaston became the Foundation's professional investment manager. The new investment strategy has worked well for the Foundation.

Dr. Gerald T. O'Mara was elected as the Board member in 1988 and served as the Chair of the Committee on Finance from 1991 to 1996. He received a M.A. in Economics from the University of Chicago and was subsequently employed by several firms. He then returned to academic economics, and was awarded a Ph.D. in Economics from Stanford University. He had become interested in Ewha University through his late wife, Kwi-Jin Lee, an English major alumna of Ewha.

With Dr. O'Mara choosing to step down as Chair of the Committee on Finance, Mr. Joseph Choong Sik Yi, a Board Member since 1976 and member of the Committee on Finance and Chair of its Budget and Finance Subcommittee, became Chair. His wife, Mrs. Soong Ok Yi, is an Ewha alumna. For many years, she served as the leader of the Chicago Chapter. Mr. Joseph Yi and his wife have been very active raising funds for various projects for Ewha University, including Eunice Lee's concerts described earlier.

The change in the management of investments, increases in stock values, and successful fundraising by the Alumnae Relations Committee (ARC) during the year of 1996 bore fruit. The Foundation received contributions totaling $250,643 in gifts and corporate matching funds. The value of the investment portfolio increased $508,666 over the year to $2,912, 647.

In 1998, Ewha alumnae gave for the first time the greatest proportion of the contributions to the Foundation, about 60% of the total of $122,040. This was a turning point as Ewha alumnae had collectively become the major source for donations. From the perspective of fundraising, it was evident Ewha alumnae had become the most fruitful sources for future contributions.

The 1999 report of the Finance Committee indicated the highest assets value in the 30-year history of the Foundation, $4,338,912.

Among the increased assets, Board members contributed $70,436, or about 20% of the year's new contributions, Ewha alumnae contributed $227,668, or about 63%, and other sources provided $61,896, or about 17%. The Foundation was able to send $239,905 including scholarships to Ewha.

The Finance Committee reported another record-breaking year in 2000 with a total assets value of $4,555,350. Of new contributions, Board members gave $33,463 or about 7%, Ewha alumnae gave $171,694, about 35%, and others provided $286,747, about 58%. The total contribution was $491,904. The Foundation sent $551,956 including scholarships to Ewha. Chair Yi noted that since its inception in 1970, this brought the total the Foundation provided the University to $3,976,001.

Figure 1 displays the annual financial contributions to the International Foundation and monetary contributions sent to Ewha during the 40 years of the Foundation's existence to 2010. The data reported in Figure 1 until about 1978 should be considered as approximations due to changes in record keeping and reporting during the Foundation's formative years. One source of data from these early years was the minutes of the Annual Meetings, in which financial reports were preliminary and not always based on a consistent fiscal year basis.

The comparison of yearly contributions to the Foundation and disbursements to Ewha during the first decades clearly show contributions greatly exceeded disbursements. This reflects the Foundation's early policy of building endowments. Years with peak contributions were typically due to special fundraising projects.

It can also be seen in Figure 1 that disbursements to Ewha increased substantially on average subsequent to a change in Foundation policy in 1999 to send more scholarship funds to Ewha. After 1999, disbursements to Ewha totaled over several years were nearly equal to contributions to the Foundation over the same time period. However, over the same time periods the Foundation assets generally increased. These increases in

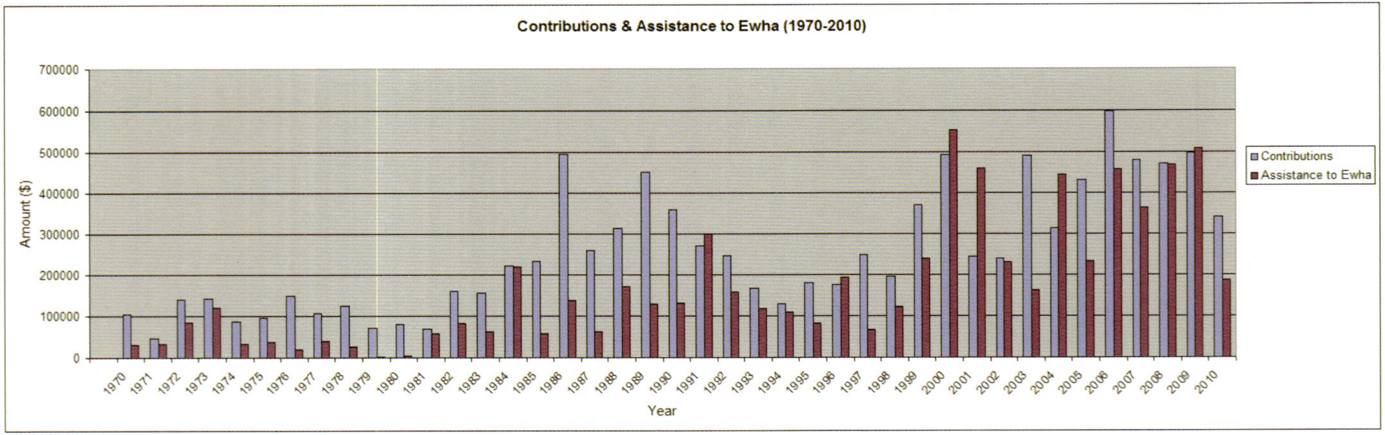

Figure 1. Annual Contributions to International Foundation and Disbursements to Ewha Womans University [International Foundation Archives]

Foundation assets largely reflected earnings resulting from solid investment management overseen by Mr. Mark Gaston, Dr. Kilchai Yim, Dr. Bumsun Lee, and others.

Outgoing Foundation Treasurer Dr. Bumsun Lee, at the 41st Annual Meeting of the Foundation in October 2010, described in his 40th and final Treasurer's report:

> *With pride, I report to you that the Ewha Foundation received contributions of 10 million dollars during these past 40 years, and has sent 7 million dollars to Ewha in Seoul, Korea. We currently have a balance of 7 million dollars....*

Such evidence showed that the International Foundation had matured into a self-sustaining and productive foundation able to provide significant and meaningful ongoing assistance to Ewha Womans University.

Part 8

Making a Difference for Ewha Students

Scholarship Disbursement

Scholarships have been an important component, but not always the highest priority, of the Ewha Cooperating Board of North America or the International Foundation that followed it. As early as September 1948, the minutes of the Ewha Cooperating Board meeting included brief discussions of scholarships. Until that time, some scholarship funding was disbursed in an ad hoc fashion. In the Board's May 1949 meeting minutes, mention was made of pending funding from the Annie Merner Pfeiffer Foundation and the setting of policy to use one-third of the funds for current scholarship expenses and two-thirds to be held in a Scholarship Endowment Fund. These first scholarships were primarily directed towards providing Ewha faculty with study opportunities in the U.S.

The onslaught of the Korean War, with the double evacuation of Ewha's Seoul campus, a temporary Busan campus, and the sudden increase in students (primarily refugees from North Korea) seeking an Ewha education, put severe strains on Ewha's viability. It was at the June

1952 Cooperating Board meeting that Miss Margaret Billingsley, Executive Secretary for Korea, brought to the attention of the Cooperating Board "the imperative need for designated scholarship funds for Christian students with the (Ewha Womans) University." It was at that seminal meeting that motions were made and passed by vote to send word out to Cooperating Mission Boards in the U.S. and Canada and to the Presbyterian Board in North America for participation in meeting the urgent need for designated scholarships for Ewha students.

The response to the request for scholarships for students attending Ewha was highly positive. The treasurer's report at the June 1954 Cooperating Board Meeting indicated that in the year April 1, 1953-March 31, 1954 the Board had sent $99,383 to Ewha University (presumably for scholarships) plus another $6,387 for supplies.

The efforts of the Cooperating Board of North America to provide scholarships for Ewha students lasted several years and set the precedence for the International Foundation to make scholarships one of its fundraising goals.

During the first decades of the Foundation, fundraising focused on supporting building construction and the equipping of facilities (for example, music instruments, science equipment, medical equipment and library books) that Ewha so urgently needed because of the growing student population. Gradually, attention was given to the provision of scholarships. These scholarships were directed initially towards students, faculty, and others whose effectiveness to serve the University would be increased by further study. For example, at the 1977 Annual Meeting of the Foundation, the Finance-Investment Committee recommended and approval was given by the Board that 70% of the income from the $56,000 Appenzeller Scholarship Fund be spent for scholarships. The first Appenzeller Scholarship was awarded shortly afterward to Professor Lee Keun-sup who was a Ph.D. candidate at Emory University.

By 1982, a Seabury Foundation gift of $7,000 and interest from investments made it possible to support the travel of several Ewha faculty for educational experiences in the U.S. Such opportunities continued with funding from the Seabury Foundation in the years to follow. In 1986, four new scholarship funds were established. In 1988, three more scholarship funds were established. By 1991, so many individual funds for undesignated scholarships had been established that they were combined into a single fund, called the *General Scholarship Fund.*

Slowly, by the mid-1990s, scholarships funds began flowing from the Foundation to support Ewha students on the Ewha campus. During the same time period, individual scholarship endowments were being established (four in 1994) as local chapters were busily establishing and growing chapter scholarship endowments residing in the Foundation. In 1996, the Foundation sent scholarship funds to Ewha that were shared by four students.

The growth of the funds residing within the Foundation were enhanced by the efforts of the Investment Sub-committee, with the portfolio reaching $3.5 million in 1997. Funds generated for scholarships were increasing at an accelerating rate. These led to a program of major disbursements of scholarship funds to Ewha Womans University.

At the 1997 Annual Meeting of the Foundation Board, Mr. Joseph Yi, Chair of the Finance Committee, pointed out that among the three responsibilities of the Finance Committee is disbursements. He said the committee had been working on a plan for disbursing scholarship funds in a way that respects the wishes of the donors and also responds to the needs of the University. A draft plan was circulated for review for consideration at the next Annual Meeting.

At the 1998 Annual Meeting, working closely with Foundation President Susanne L. Stevens, Mr. Yi presented the scholarship disbursement recommendations. They were approved by the Board. Mrs. Stevens and Mr. Yi immediately led the first major scholarship disbursement totaling $125,000. From 1998 to 2000 over $600,000 of scholarships was given to Ewha students. This was a historic accomplishment for the Foundation, and demonstrated a high priority for scholarship support by both the Foundation and donors, mostly alumnae, alumnae families, and local alumnae associations.

Among the first scholarships given were to two candidates who were nominated by Ewha: Choi Yoo-kyung for the P. William Lee Memorial Scholarship, and Kim Ye-jin for the Marion Conrow Memorial Scholarship. The first Susan Ruby Lamb Memorial Scholarship was granted to Park Minjung for a general scholarship for her graduate course in regional research.

The dramatic growth in the number of scholarships supported by endowments marked a major turning point for the Foundation. The growth was possible through the excellent leadership of the Investment Subcommittee members Mr. Mark Gaston, Dr. Kilchai Yim, and Dr. Bumsun Lee. Also, the Alumnae Relations Committee (ARC), led by Dr. Soon Ja Choi, and local chapters played major roles resulting in the establishment and growing of scholarship endowments. The emergence of scholarships as the major means of support to Ewha was evidenced when Mr. Joseph C. Yi, Chair, International Education and Cultural Exchange, announced the awarding of $310,000 for scholarships in 2000. The Committee approved the practice of providing awards to be given in $5,000 grants. At the time, annual tuition at Ewha was $5,000.

Celebrating Thirty Years of the International Foundation: 1999

The International Foundation celebrated its 30th Annual Foundation Meeting in Chicago in November 1999. The meeting was called to order by President Susanne Stevens. Highlighting the first day of the meeting were annual reports by the presidents of the Foundation and the University. President Stevens, in her Annual Report of the Foundation, described the Foundation's progress, especially noting that 1999 represented a strong year of scholarship support. She then posed what she considered to be two challenges in the years ahead: First, improvement in the flow of funds and scholarships to Ewha; Second, transition of Foundation leadership to Korean-Americans. She suggested that accomplishment of these challenges will require a cohesive communication process among the Board members, alumnae, friends of Ewha, and the Foundation.

When presenting her Annual Report of the University to the group, Ewha President Chang Sang expressed her heartiest appreciation to the Foundation for its continuing contributions to the University's needs. She also reminded the audience of " ... our foremothers who dreamed dreams for women's education in the Land of the Morning Calm, and so Ewha was born. ... Today Ewha has the mission of contributing to the development of women and humanity worldwide ... we will do all in our power to fulfill that enormous responsibility and mission ..." Almost like a quickening and crescendoing drumbeat, a message was being conveyed by the University leadership that the time had arrived when Ewha was not only the beneficiary of a *River of Faith* but also the channel through which the *River of Faith* flows deeper, wider, and stronger to women and humanity beyond Korea's borders.

Mr. Joseph C. Yi, as Chair of the Committee of International Education and Culture Exchange in 1999, expressed poignantly the series of events leading up the 30th year of the Foundation. He repeated what he had stated many times before, perhaps with the hope of making it into a mantra for the International Foundation so no one can forget,

> *... The purpose of the Foundation was, and it still is, to raise funds in America and send them to Ewha to fill the various needs of the University.*

The 30th International Foundation Annual Meeting can be examined to exhibit common and unique elements of such meetings until recent years. Currently, the annual meetings of the Foundation and the Ewha Womans University United Alumnae Chapters of North America typically take place in the same location on the same weekend, but are programmatically scheduled separately with Foundation Board members invited to the alumnae association's banquet. Wherever the Annual Meeting is held, the local alumnae association serves as host, assists in making the arrangements for the meeting venue and provides information on lodging and local travel for the meeting attendees. Board members and others attending the meeting cover their own travel expenses, including lodging and meals. Fellowship and the nurturing of the Ewha spirit is always part of the Annual Meeting.

Fundraising has often been part of the annual gathering, depending on the local chapter interests and capabilities. On the day before the opening of this November 1999 Foundation meeting, there was a private fundraising $500/plate dinner party. The purpose was to raise funds for scholarships to be placed in the Chicago's portion of the Foundation's scholarship portfolio, which would fund scholarships for Ewha students, funds for continuing education for the Ewha faculty, and other programs to be determined by the Chicago Ewha Alumnae Association.

The goal was to have a 40-person event. Fifty-eight people attended the dinner and the net proceeds were $26,032. These proceeds were placed in the Chicago Ewha Alumnae Association Fund.

Each year, the star attraction at the Annual Meeting is the President of the University if she is able to attend. Understandably, everyone wants to see, hear, touch and greet the President. President Chang Sang delivered a wonderful message to the Chicago alumnae and to the Meeting audience.

At this Annual Meeting, as with other Annual Meetings, the Foundation's Executive Committee first meets. The Executive Committee consists of the President, the Vice Presidents, and the Chairs of Committees. Then the main meeting commences with a plenary session, followed by the Committee meetings. In all, there are five committees: The Finance and Investment Committee, the Committee on Fundraising and Promotion, the Committee on International Education and Cultural Exchange, the Committee on Nomination, and the Alumnae Relations Committee.

A Dinner with the President, hosted by the University, ends the first day. It provides an opportunity for its President to express her appreciation to the Foundation for all that it does for the University.

The second day of the meeting for the Board members starts with the business meeting. After roll call and approval of the Minutes of the previous year's Meeting, the President of the Foundation (Mrs. Susan L. Stevens in 1999) and the University president (Dr. Chang Sang) give their annual reports. The following describes the rest of the meeting as it played out.

Dr. Bumsun Lee delivered the Treasurer's report, and the reports of the other committees were presented by their chairs. Included in the process was the approval of the Operations Budget for the fiscal year 2000.

A significant point was made that, for the second year in a row, the donations of Ewha alumnae to the Foundation were greater than the donations from the non-alumnae sector. Another milestone was that the Foundation granted funds for more than 60 scholarships to Ewha students. As of the end of the fiscal year 1999, the Foundation fund balance stood at $4,338,912. The Foundation sent to Ewha a total $529,506 in the time period October 1, 1999 to June 30, 2000.

During the Alumnae Relations Committee (ARC) report, each local Ewha alumnae association reported its activities and presented their donations to the Foundation's Ewha Alumnae Association Funds. Eighty-five alumnae were present, coming from as far away as Alaska.

The last item on the agenda was the announcement of the site of the next year's annual meeting.

The day ended with the 30th Annual Banquet hosted by the Chicago Alumnae Association, and to which the Board members were invited.

Part 9

Launching the 21st Century

"Remembering the Past ... Imagine for the Future"

Entering the fourth decade of its existence, and with the Year 2000 soon to arrive, caused many to reflect on the International Foundation's role in the phenomenal growth of Ewha Womans University. The Foundation could justly be proud of the assistance it provided to Ewha when it was so badly needed for constructing buildings, equipping facilities, providing faculty enhancement, and funding scholarships. Such reflection could only fuel enthusiasm among the Foundation leadership and Ewha alumnae to seek new ways of benefiting Ewha's mission of educating women to become effective and empowered members and leaders in modern society worldwide.

At the November 2000 Annual Meeting of the Foundation, Ewha President Chang Sang described what she saw as a shifting paradigm of the role of women that was reflected in the University, in Korea, and in the world. The new paradigm encompassed: 1) The emerging role of women embodied with their abilities of flexibility and sensitivity; 2)

The age of information requiring that Ewha stay current and continue its collaboration in the area of research and development; 3) Globalization leading to changing employment practices and competition; and, 4) Unification of North and South Korea through emerging joint programs.

President Chang encouraged the audience to be cognizant of possible creative initiatives before they become "lost opportunities," mentioning that Chinese universities were providing support for North Korean women. She also called for moves "beyond national borders" in the areas of research and professional education, as well as building networks within society. She pointed out that Ewha continues to host international conferences for women throughout Asia.

Highlights at the meeting included the announcement by Mr. Joseph Yi, Chair of the International Education and Cultural Exchange Committee, that the total scholarship funding to be sent to Ewha in 2000 was $210,000.

The new President of the Foundation, Mrs. Hannah C. Meadors, as she related in her President's Annual Report of the Foundation at the 2000 Annual Meeting, was a relative newcomer to the Foundation who wanted to learn about the history of Ewha University in the context of Korean history. Mrs. Meadors stressed "Remembering the Past ... Imagine for the Future." She applauded the wisdom and spirit of the early founders of the University for their commitment to the education and liberation of young women in Korea. She took note of the historical connection between the Methodist Church and Ewha. She thanked the "giants of the past," and then moved to the present by identifying Ewha President Chang as "the" imagination of today. She cited alumnae, Board members, and scholarship awardees who also reflect imagination. Finally, she shared examples "to imagine" ... the International Foundation president's gavel being handed to a Korean-American and ... and the vision of a unified Korea.

Mrs. Hannah Campbell Meadors joined the Foundation in 1998 as a Board member and served as President from 2000 to 2002. In 2002 she stepped down from the presidency due to illness and passed away in 2003. Her tenure, although short, was a time of significant progress for the Foundation.

7th President, IFEWU,
Mrs. Hannah Meadors
[International Foundation Archives]

Her professional career focused on early childhood education and children in poverty.

She was Director of Early Childhood Development in the Education Division of the Office of Governor Richard Riley, South Carolina. Rust College, Holly Springs, Mississippi awarded her the Honorary Doctor of Humanities degree for her humanitarian services. She served on the Task Force for the Bishops Initiative on Children and Poverty and was an advocate for meeting the needs of children in Macedonia and villages in Kosovo, Russia, Africa, Mexico and Palestine. Her husband, United Methodist Bishop Marshall Jack Meadors, served in church capacities in South Carolina and Mississippi.

The Year 2001 was an eventful year in many respects. It started with joyful news from Ewha President Chang Sang. By letter, she informed the Foundation that:

> *In March 2001, Ewha ranked first in the Ministry of Education's overall evaluation of 182 universities in Korea. Specifically, Ewha proved most excellent in the quality of education, education reform policy and its implementation, and transparent financial management. It is truly a shocking news for Korea's male-centered society to learn that a women's university was recognized the best university in our nation, surpassing renowned co-ed institutions such as Seoul National University, Yonsei and Korea University. Again, we cannot but recall with heartfelt*

appreciation the Foundation's supportive role which has helped our university achieve so much.

Foundation President Meadors rejoiced in conveying the exciting news to Foundation Board members, Ewha alumnae, and friends of Ewha. She wrote:

Our hearts rejoice at this good news and we are reminded of those who paved the way by risking their lives, in many instances, to make Ewha a reality. ... we pay homage to those who had the dream, who remembered the past, and who were determined to change the future of women in Korea through Christian education. We give thanks for visionaries such as Mary F. Scranton, the Methodist missionary who founded Ewha in 1886, for Lulu E. Frey, Dr. Alice R. Appenzeller, and Dr. Helen Kim. We recognize the effort and sacrifice of faculty, staff, students, alumnae, and friends of Ewha who tirelessly worked to bring the image of Korean women from one of servitude to agents of change in leadership roles. And, of course we proudly lift our own President Sang Chang as a shining example of vision and imagination for the new millennium.

These comments were delivered via a May Day letter in which she announced the creation of a May Day Fund that had been proposed by Mrs. Margaret Moore and Mrs. Shirley Jeffery, members of the Committee on Fundraising and Promotion. Mrs. Moore was a missionary who had taught at Ewha for many years. She felt that the time of celebrating Ewha's beginning was an excellent time to ask for funds to help students in financial need. The appeal letter was sent to alumnae, friends, and Foundation members. The purpose was to set up scholarships providing temporary assistance to Ewha students who were most at risk of dropping out of school due to financial stress, while joyfully noting the anniversary of Ewha's founding.

In the first May Day (2002) letter, President Meadors made the case for giving to scholarships directed towards students with financial emergencies. She wrote:

> *... in March 2001, Ewha ranked first in the Ministry of Education's overall evaluation of 182 Universities in Korea. ... Founders Day gives us the opportunity to say thank you to all those who helped make Ewha the University it is today. Ewha is a gift to Korea and all the world, providing broad educational opportunities for girls and women ... We are proposing that a MAY DAY FUND be established for Ewha, the purpose of which is to provide temporary assistance to students who are in danger of having to drop out of school due to financial stress. It is crucial that we help those young women complete their Ewha education. ...*

As a result of this appeal, a total of $8,433 was earmarked for Ewha in 2002. May Day Fund appeal letters have been sent out by the Foundation President each year since 2002.

Not all of 2001 was about good news. The International Foundation was, as was all of America, impacted by the September 11, 2001 terrorist attack in the U.S. In a 2001 issue of *Ewha News*, President Meadors wrote of her deep concern on the morning of September 11th when she received an email from Foundation Executive Director, Mrs. Ji-yei Song Park, who was working in the Foundation's Manhattan office, which ended, "I will have to stop now. We are being evacuated from the building." Mrs. Meadors immediately turned on the television to learn of the immensity of the situation in lower Manhattan and elsewhere. It was hours later that Mrs. Park emailed that she was safely back in the Foundation office. Although it took much longer than usual, she was able to make it home that day.

All of the U.S. was shrouded in a fog of fear that spread almost instantly from the Al-Qaeda impact sites in New York, Washington, DC, and Shanksville, Pennsylvania. President Meadors sought to inspire Board members, Ewha alumnae, and friends of Ewha, asking them to remain united to hold high the principles of freedom for young women and the world. She called for energy to pursue the tasks that faced the Foundation. She wrote, "I am grateful for Ewha University. In a sense, she is the Statue of Liberty and holds high the light for the future. I am grateful for the Foundation. We can provide the energy to keep the light burning brightly. United, we will stand."

The Foundation demonstrated its resilience as it continued to support Ewha. Mr. Mark Gaston's professional asset management that diversified Foundation investments assured budgetary stability and Foundation sustainability. The 2000 report had recorded the highest assets value ($4,555,350) in the history of the Foundation up to that time.

Ewha alumnae contributions gave ample evidence of the growing participation in Foundation fundraising. The Alumnae Relations Committee (ARC) made remarkable inroads in reaching out to alumnae all over North America. The *Ewha News* publication reflected the Foundation's recognition of the growing roles of alumnae and local alumnae chapters, including their fundraising potential, by going bilingual.

Revering Ewha in a Personal Way

At the Foundation's Annual Meeting in November 1999, Ewha President Chang Sang asked for help in acquiring funds for the renovation of the Welch-Ryang Auditorium. The Auditorium had been erected and dedicated on the occasion of Ewha's 70th Anniversary, May 31, 1956, in honor of the valuable services rendered by Bishop Herbert Welch, the first Resident Bishop in Korea of the Methodist Episcopal Church, United States of America, and Bishop Ju Sam Ryang, the first Korean Bishop of the Korean Methodist Episcopal Church. The Welch-Ryang Auditorium was built with the help from the Board of Global Mission of The

Methodist Church and the Ewha Cooperating Board of North America. The well-used building was badly in need of modernization.

In response to President Chang's request, a unique fundraising approach was employed jointly by the Fundraising and Promotion Committee and the Alumnae Relations Committee (ARC).

Donations were solicited to pay for individual chairs for the Auditorium. For about a year beginning in 2000, a mail and telephone campaign was conducted asking individuals to consider paying $800 for a chair and local alumnae associations were requested to buy chairs at the rate of $1,000 per chair. The offer proved especially attractive because the gift of chairs was tangible. A plaque was placed on each chair identifying the donor and to whom the chair was dedicated if that was the donor's wish. It is known that in the years that followed, many donors visiting their alma mater especially enjoyed looking for their chairs.

It was reported by the coordinator of the Foundation's campaign that $120,000 was raised for 150 chairs. In total, at least 247 individuals and

Donated chairs in Welch-Ryang Auditorium renovation [Ewha Archives]

15 local alumnae chapters contributed towards the purchase of chairs.

Many donors expressed their love for Ewha through their donations. Mr. and Mrs. Pearl Pyung-ok and Lester Kim donated $1,600 for two chairs in memory of Bishop Herbert Welch and Bishop J. S. Ryang. The Kims were living in California at the time, so they were able to attend the Ewha Alumnae Association Annual Banquet at Anaheim, California in 2000. Mrs. Kim told of being overjoyed to share her *River of Faith* through their precious contribution for the chairs. According to Mrs. Kim, she worked very hard in rehabilitation to recover from a stroke so she could teach piano to students. The earnings from her teaching went towards their donation. Both of the Bishops were friends of Mrs. Kim's parents and Bishop Welch had officiated at their wedding.

Word of the chair campaign was spread by alumnae around the country. One such person, Mrs. Seon Choo Chung Kim, President of the St. Louis Ewha Alumnae Association, called many alumnae friends all over the U.S. to encourage participation in memory of loved ones and to honor Ewha.

Another moving story came from Mrs. Susanne Ellis, who contributed a chair in memory of her husband. Her late husband, Dr. Howard W. Ellis, participated in a 1961 religious campaign at Ewha led by Dr. Harry Denman, a Methodist evangelist. They preached and baptized 1,200 girls in the Welch-Ryang Auditorium.

The Welch-Ryang Auditorium chair project provided much more than direct support to Ewha. The broad-based appeal awakened strong feelings of attachment and rich memories among alumnae and friends of Ewha. For many, this first material contribution to their beloved alma mater set the stage for future giving.

The Foundation supported Ewha with a total of $480,059 from July 1, 2000 to June 30, 2001, according to the Summer 2001 issue of *Ewha News*. Included in that time period was $68,550 from the Auditorium Renovation (chair) Project.

The Foundation Imagines for the Future

Ewha's 12th President Shin In-ryung [Ewha Archives]

Ewha Womans University entered the 21st century in an enviable position, having been ranked first in the Ministry of Education's March 2001 overall evaluation of 182 universities in Korea.

In August 2002, Dr. Shin In-ryung became the 12th President of Ewha Womans University. She addressed the 33rd Foundation Annual Board Meeting in November 2002 and expressed her deep appreciation of the assistance received from the Foundation. She then described the University's Development Planning tasks established for facing the 21st century. They included: 1) Reduction of numbers of students being admitted; 2) Improvement in quality of education and research; 3) Enhancement of the foundation for better research and specialization; 4) Improvement of the campus environment; 5) Creation of a better academic environment; 6) Attraction of talented students; 7) Implementation of projects such as Life Sciences; and, 8) Preparation for Ewha University's 120th Founding Anniversary. According to President Shin, the challenges that Ewha faces for the 21st century deal with space for building research facilities and for accommodating increasing numbers of students and teaching faculty. The immediate challenge was that by 2005 the student population was projected to be 22,000.

The Foundation, under President Meadors' leadership, was also thinking ahead. She had established a Master Plan Task Force in late 2001 and charged it to examine the strengths of the Foundation and challenges being faced by the Foundation in the years ahead.

Fortuitously, the Master Plan Task Force creation coincided with the appointment of a new Executive Director. Recommended by Board Treasurer Dr. Bumsun Lee, Mrs. Ji-yei Song Park was hired in 2001. Mrs. Park's affiliation with Ewha dates back to her undergraduate and graduate studies. She received her bachelor's degree in 1986 and her master's degree in 1988, both in Christian Studies. She accepted a highly coveted internship with the World Alliance of Reformed Churches at their headquarters in Geneva, Switzerland. She studied theology at Bern University for two years. Mrs. Park worked as a staff member in the office of the President of Ewha University until 1998. Her deep ties to Ewha and her study and work experiences provided excellent preparation for her new position.

Her extensive background enabled Mrs. Park to quickly assume the responsibilities of the office and execute the multiple tasks of the executive directorship, including running the office, maintaining financial records, assisting in fundraising tasks, preparation of *Ewha Foundation News*, communications with the Board members, Ewha alumnae, and friends of Ewha. Communications with Ewha alumnae were increasingly important as the numbers of alumnae in North America was thought to be more than 10,000 in year 2000.

Foundation Executive Director
Mrs. Ji-yei Song Park
[International Foundation Archives]

The Foundation Master Plan Task Force worked through much of 2002 to identify Foundation achievements and strengths, then identify current and future challenges, and finally, propose ways to implement change. The Task Force members were Hai Won Chang, Sung Hak Lee Choi, Mark Gaston, Hwain Chang Lee, Chang Hyun Shin Geer, Bumsun Lee, Soyoung Lee J. D., Suncha Lim Lee, Jane Oh, and Maxwell Rhee. Tuckie Yirchott and Ex officio were Hannah Meadors, Kilchai Yim, Joseph Yi, and Tuckie Yirchott.

Task Force members identified the Foundation achievements and strengths since its founding 33 years before: 1) A strong Board of Directors member involvement; 2) Increased scholarship endowments; 3) A strong working relationship between the Foundation and Ewha University, working closely with Ewha administration and Ewha alumnae; and, 4) A good track record of fund raising, such as obtaining grants.

The challenges the Task Force identified included: 1) Development of a greater role for the Foundation to strengthen ties between Ewha and its alumnae in North America; 2) Raising more funds from individuals, foundations, and institutions; 3) Assisting Ewha in meeting the goals of Ewha's *Vision 21*, such as globalization for its programs and educational missions; 4) Going beyond the focus on financial assistance for Ewha; 5) Increasing involvement of Ewha alumnae in Foundation's activities; and, 6) Implementing several structural changes to the Board organization to meet changing times.

Master Plan Task Force [International Foundation Archives]

During the tenure of the Task Force, several tasks were identified and implementation initiated almost immediately. The Foundation created the Foundation website, a Foundation logo, a handbook for the Foundation, a new Foundation brochure, and a plan for a biennial fundraising event sponsored by the Foundation. Considerable amounts of individual and group effort went into implementing these tasks.

Foundation brochure with new logo
[International Foundation Archives]

The first *Handbook of the International Foundation for Ewha Womans University, Inc.* was prepared by Dr. Chang Hyun Shin Geer, primarily for use by Board members and others as a reference to better understand the Foundation, to have knowledge of its history, and to have a guide for current work and relationships. It was first employed to orient new Board members at the 33rd Annual Meeting in November 2002. The *Handbook* was revised in 2009 by Dr. Moon Ja Chung Park.

A Foundation website was conceived, created, and placed online. It was a breakthrough communication tool for the Foundation. It has since been expanded and modified as warranted (Address: www.ewhafoundation.org). A unique Foundation logo was conceptualized by Dr. Chang Hyun Shin Geer, Dr. Hai Won Chang and Mr. John Y. Geer (Dr. Shin Geer's son). The logo visualized the partnership of Ewha in Korea and the International Foundation in North America. It first appeared in 2002, replacing the Ewha University logo the Foundation had employed since 1970.

A Foundation fundraising brochure was developed, printed, and distributed with the support of a Seabury Foundation grant of $10,000. Mrs. Shirley Jeffery, Dr. Chang Hyun Shin Geer, and Ms. Soyoung Lee, J. D., created the brochure, *Join by Giving, Ewha's Vision 21, – to enlighten, educate, empower women in Korea and worldwide –*. The brochure invited recipients to contribute towards an Ewha Womans University's program to help build a world in which women are empowered and their values and achievements matter. The brochure was designed to elicit support for a particular Ewha program directed towards the expansion of the University's mission abroad. At the same time, perhaps of equal or greater importance, it was intended to inform Ewha alumnae of the ways contributions can conveniently be made to their beloved alma mater through the Foundation.

These and other outcomes from the Task Force that had been established under President Meadors' leadership were significant, forward looking, and lasting. It was with sadness that President Meador's tenure was cut short due to her illness. In the brief time she led the Foundation, she made her mark. Her contributions added to those of many others who came before her, and strengthened the flow of the Ewha *River of Faith*.

Student Appreciation of Foundation Scholarships

The concerns and support that you (the contributors of Foundation scholarships) have bestowed on the students of Ewha all this time have always given us consolation ....

Foundation President Meadors and recipients of 2002 Foundation scholarships
[International Foundation Archives]

These were the words of a recipient during a May 2002 ceremony of scholarship presentations by Foundation President Hannah Meadors and Board members Dr. Hai Won Chang, Mrs. Mi Hwa Yoo Hong, and Mrs. Seon Choo Chung Kim, who were participating in the 116th Anniversary of the Founding of Ewha on the University campus.

President Meadors and the Board Members were deeply moved by the opportunity to meet Foundation scholarship recipients in person and by the receipt of lovely thank-you notes.

The scholarship amounts sent to Ewha depend greatly on the availability of funds during the particular year. For example, the scholarship funds disbursed were $125,000 in 1999, $310,000 in 2000, and $188,000 in 2001. In 2001, 48 students were awarded Foundation scholarships.

Scholarship funds are sent yearly to the University, where the Student Personnel Office manages the scholarship selection process. As a courtesy, the scholarship recipients usually write thank-you letters to the donors that are sent through the International Foundation office.

Other examples of appreciation letters written by recipients follow:

Eom Soohyun: Mark Gaston Scholarship.

I am deeply grateful to you for granting me the Mark Gaston Scholarship for Ewha Womans University. I was really pleased at the news. It is a great honor for me to be a fellowship recipient of your Foundation. I will work hard for the rest of my college days to make achievements which are worthy of the honor. You truly inspired me to further efforts. I will do my best to meet your expectation. And just as I was supported by you, I will continuously help other people who are in need. Thank you again for your help.

Choi Jin-Seon: Whilsmith Memorial Scholarship.

When I was in high School, my teacher told us a variety of coverage about our social problems and suggested participating in social movements. Since then, my interest increased which led me to major social sciences. I chose this major because I thought if I know about social problems and how to solve them, I can make a better society in the future ... My father died when I was 12, due to cerebral hemorrhage. Since then, my mom solely supported our family. This year, with the scholarship, I hope I can lessen her burden and become independent ... .

International Foundation Biennial Fundraisers: 2003-2009

Another recommendation arising from the 2002 Task Force was the promotion of major fundraising events. The first Foundation fundraising event was held on April 29, 2003 at the Yale Club in New York City. The

2003 First Biennial Fundraising Dinner, New York [International Foundation Archives]

event was co-chaired by Board members Dr. Hwain Chang Lee and Mr. Mark Gaston. The Dinner event was honored by the participation of Dr. Chung Ii-sook, the emeritus Chair of Ewha Haktang, Dr. James T. Laney and Mr. Donald Gregg, both former U.S. Ambassadors to Korea.

Dr. Laney gave a moving speech describing in historical context the immense contribution Ewha made and continues to make to the benefit of women and the larger society, in which he said:

> *Ewha almost single-handedly raised the profile of women in Korea and opened the doors of opportunity for them across society ... Moving beyond the traditional roles for women, to such as teaching and nursing, medicine and law and engineering ..., Ewha quietly and effectively revolutionized society ... .*

Dr. Betty S. Mitchell, President of the Foundation from 1971 to 1978, and Dr. Kilchai Yim, who served as the Foundation's Vice

President from 1981 to 2002, were honored. The gratitude of Ewha Womans University for their significant contributions was expressed by Dr. Chung Ii-sook.

The Dinner successfully promoted the International Foundation's call for support. Over 150 guests participated and the event was honored by the presence of members of the United Board for Christian Higher Education in Asia. The event brought in an initial contribution of more than $50,000. It was hoped the fundraising event would draw corporate participation. Invitations to more than 100 corporations were met with minimal response.

The second major Foundation Biennial Fundraising Dinner was carried out in the Washington, DC area. It was organized by local Foundation Board members and the local Ewha Alumnae Association at the Marriott Hotel in Rockville, Maryland on April 24, 2005. The theme was Ewha's *Vision 21* and the event was held to raise funds for the Ewha Campus Complex to be completed in May 2006 and for scholarship support. Mrs. Yaun Dahm Yoo Han, former Foundation Board member, Ms. Chunhae Hong Yang, President of Ewha Alumnae Association of Greater Washington, and Mrs. Myungji Lee Han led the event. The highly successful event raised approximately $50,000.

The Third Biennial Fundraising Dinner was held on April 28, 2007 at the Garden Suite Hotel, Los Angeles, California. Ms. Sook Hyun Lee, Dr. Jong H. Lee and Mrs. Suncha Lim Lee coordinated the program. Ms. Sook Hyun Lee worked with the Los Angeles-based fundraising Dinner Committee. The keynote speaker was Mrs. Harriet Fulbright, president of the J. William and Harriet Fulbright Center. Mrs. Fulbright had taught in Ewha's English Department from 1958 to 1960. Ms. Fulbright was elected as an honoree of the Foundation. In her presentation she spoke of the importance of the global village, and she placed Ewha in its world context:

2005 Second Biennial Fundraising Dinner, Washington, DC [International Foundation Archives]

2007 Third Biennial Fundraising Dinner, Los Angeles [International Foundation Archives]

When I taught there (Ewha Womans University) almost fifty years ago, there was a real curiosity among the students about the world outside of the Korean peninsula. Always a leader in the education of young women, it has within the last few decades embraced international studies and added interdisciplinary courses to introduce its students to the new trends and ideas being explored in other parts of the world. It is justifiably proud of its 120-years history and is determined to maintain its preeminence as a first rate university … .

The number of attendees for the Fundraising Dinner was 134. The net income of the fundraiser was $33,000.

The Fourth Biennial Fundraising Dinner, held on April 15, 2010 in the New York area, was also the celebration of the International Foundation's first 40 years. A total of nearly $100,000 was donated, with another $450,000 promised in pledges to the Helen Kim Society.

Part 10

Ensuring Partnerships in the 21st Century

Abiding Commitment for Partnership

The Year 2003 was both sad and joyous for the Foundation. The Foundation lost a dedicated friend with the passing of President Hannah Meadors, who had touched many by her vision and humanity. The new President, Bishop Sharon Z. Rader, uplifted the Foundation and the Board was reassured by her presence.

Bishop Sharon Zimmerman Rader graduated from North Central College in 1961 and taught in Michigan, Ohio, and New Jersey. She did graduate work at the University of Michigan and Eastern Michigan University. She later graduated from Garrett Evangelical Theological Seminary. Adrian College awarded her with an honorary doctorate in 1989.

She was elected to the United Methodist Church Episcopacy by the North Central Jurisdictional Conference in 1992 and assigned to the Wisconsin Area. From 1996 to 2004 she served as Secretary of the Council of Bishops. As of 2011, she was serving as the Ecumenical Officer for the Council of Bishops.

8th President, IFEWU,
Bishop Sharon Z. Rader
[International Foundation Archives]

Bishop Rader's path to the International Foundation was paved by Mrs. Hannah Meadors. Bishop Rader first met Mrs. Meadors in Lake Junaluska, NC when Hannah's husband, Bishop Jack Marshall Meadors, Bishop Ann Sherer-Simpson, and she were attending leadership training. The three of them were elected Bishops in 1992.

Later, Bishop Rader told Mrs. Meadors of her interest in Ewha because she had visited Korea, had given a lecture at Ewha, and was impressed by the vibrant University community. Mrs. Meadors asked her to become a Foundation Board Member, and she accepted the invitation. Later, at the request of her dear friend, Hannah Meadors, Bishop Rader graciously accepted the Presidency of the International Foundation.

In her Annual President's Report at the 34th Annual Meeting held in San Francisco in November 2003, Bishop Rader addressed the theme, "We've come this far by faith."

> *God's never failed us yet. How true. Whether the path we walk is one of beauty or of struggle, God joins us in the journey. ... God has been with this Foundation in the past year as we have celebrated and mourned, as we have been discouraged and hoped, as we have wandered and renewed our commitment. We've come this far by faith ... God never failed us yet!*

With these words, the Board Members were encouraged and inspired to imagine the future. All expressed a sense of renewed commitment for helping Ewha.

During the same time period, Ewha was moving forward under the leadership of its new President, Dr. Shin In-ryung. While the U.S. was continuing to struggle with its responses to the September 11, 2001 attacks, Korea saw the need to deal with rapid changes enmeshed with global interrelationships. President Shin announced Ewha's intent to move forward with enrichment through global partnerships by developing the Ewha Global Partnership Program (EGPP). A fundamental component would be the provision of scholarships enabling women from developing countries in Southeast Asia, Africa and Latin America to study at Ewha to prepare them for leadership roles in their own countries. This planned program clearly demonstrated Ewha's goal to enlighten, educate, empower women in Korea and worldwide.

The Year 2003 was bountiful in terms of the Foundation's fundraising and financial picture. The Foundation's net assets approached the $5 million mark and $491,000 was raised to help build the endowment base for scholarships. Over $163,000 was sent to Ewha for 60 scholarships. The progress resulting from the implementation of the recent Task Force report was evident. In particular, the dedicated work by Dr. Hwain Chang Lee and Mr. Mark Gaston to host the exquisite Fundraising Dinner in April 2003 was a major contribution towards making the Foundation a more aggressive fundraising organization.

Advancing the Role of Women in Medicine in the Global Society

Ewha Womans University's College of Medicine, founded after World War II, has become one of the top-ranking medical schools in Korea. Its goal has been to constantly grow and excel through expansion of programs. In support of that goal, a Medical Research Fund was established in 1995 within the Foundation's Alumni Relations Committee (ARC) via its Medical Support Committee, co-chaired by Ewha Medical College graduates Dr. Yong Ok Cho and Dr. Ok Hee Won. Its goal was

Mokdong Hospital [Ewha Archives]

to build a $200,000 endowment. Its purpose was to support important projects such as expanding Medical College facilities, funding research programs, modernizing medical equipment, and generating scholarships. By 2000, $50,000 had been generated, and by September 2004, the total amount of contributions was $103,729. Of that, $14,600 had been contributed in fiscal year 2004.

Board member and Alumnae Relations Committee (ARC) member Dr. Moonja Chung Park embarked on a new round of solicitations for the Medical Research Fund in 2004. With the theme "Power of One," Dr. Park led a campaign asking Ewha College of Medicine alumnae to act on the Ewha motto of "Respect and Sharing" by helping their alma mater achieve the highest world standards of medical education.

As part of the fundraising activity, Dr. Park compiled and published a North American medical school graduate directory. She distributed the directory with a solicitation letter, in which she conveyed the following:

The Medical College of Ewha Womans University is making strides in our students' education to embrace the globalization of our society. However, school financing alone is insufficient to support our renowned medical school facilities and research programs. This is the opportune time for the alumnae to actively contribute.

Her message informed alumnae that they could ensure that future graduates will have the confidence and ability as medical professionals to help people live healthier lives. The response was positive, with another $12,500 being added to the Fund in fiscal year 2005. By 2007, the total contributions to the Medical Research Fund had reached $166,086. Dr. Park continued the campaign for additional funds into the following years. The goal of $200,000 was successfully reached in 2010, and annual payments to Ewha College of Medicine (or Medical School) were started. The first remittance was $20,000 in 2011.

Alumnae's Expanding Role in Fundraising

Ewha alumna have collectively become a major force in the Foundation's fundraising on Ewha's behalf. While the endowments, contributions, and fundraising efforts of the Board members and friends of Ewha continued, the Alumnae Relations Committee (ARC) gave focus to fundraising by alumnae and alumnae associations.

The surge of immigration and the improved economic status of Korean Americans through successful academic, professional and business careers increased the pool of Ewha alumnae financially able to make contributions to the benefit of Ewha.

The Alumnae Relations Committee (ARC), under the leadership of Mrs. Suncha Lim Lee and Mrs. Heesung Lee Chough, showed strong team spirit in developing and implementing fundraising strategies. In the process, ARC developed a database of 5,000 alumnae which strongly en-

Executive Committee members at 2005 Annual Board Meeting [International Foundation Archives]

hanced the capacity for communicating and fundraising.

The attendance of Ewha alumnae at Foundation Annual Meetings increased in 2004 when the Houston Alumnae Association simultaneously hosted the now-called Ewha Womans University United Alumnae Chapters of North America on November 11-13, 2004 in Houston, Texas. Fifteen chapters and 99 alumnae participated in the Annual meeting of the alumnae chapters partnering with the International Foundation's annual meeting.

At the International Foundation's 36th Annual Meeting hosted by the Cleveland Alumnae Association in November 2005, Ewha President Shin In-ryung gave the annual President's report. She described the University's ongoing Development Planning that emphasized restructuring. Basically, both quantity and quality were being addressed. Fewer students were to be enrolled, while increasing the recruitment of the most talented students. Focus was to be on improving the physical environment, including incorporation of the latest 21st century technology.

President Shin described the Ewha Campus Complex – a futuristic, grand-scale campus valley then being built as part of Ewha's *Vision 21*. The Ewha Campus Complex was designed as basically two underground buildings facing each other across a huge open-air walkway, forming a spacious valley that delivers sunlight to subterranean spaces. The complex puts in one location student meeting, lounge and study places, classrooms, computer labs, cafeterias, restaurants, and numerous retail shops, as well as parking facilities. The Center's completion was expected to help resolve the University's chronic problems of overcrowding and lack of facilities while retaining a spacious landscaped campus appearance. Ewha University was campaigning for $100 million to build the Center, with the bulk coming from Korean businesses and other in-country sources.

Friends, Board members of the Foundation and Ewha alumnae were invited to contribute via the Foundation's ECC (Ewha Campus Complex) Fund. Notably, Foundation Board Member Dr. Soon-Young Yoon contributed $140,000 toward the ECC Fund. President Shin expressed hope for the Center's completion by Ewha's 120th Anniversary, Founder's Day, May 2006. It was actually completed a year later. With its opening, it immediately became a centerpiece of campus life and an emblem of Ewha's forward thinking.

Dr. Soon-Young Yoon
[International Foundation Archives]

During Dr. Shin In-ryung's tenure as Ewha's president, the University planned and initiated the Ewha Global Partnership Program (EGPP) with the goal of educating students from developing countries to become professionals and global leaders. President Shin wrote in her letter announcing the launching of the EGPP:

Ewha Campus Complex [Photo by Yoon Suk-joon]

... Ewha's mission has always been to prepare young women for their productive roles in society and the world. Today, Ewha Womans University is the largest women's university in the world with 23,000 students, 14 colleges and 14 graduate schools. Ewha has also expanded women's opportunities for higher education, contributed to the modernization of Korean society, and the improvement of women's lives through active social participation. ... As the pioneering force in women's education, Ewha dreams to expand its educational efforts in service to the world. In this spirit, we are establishing the EGPP scholarship to sow new seeds of hope for women in the world as (Methodist missionary and Ewha founder) Mrs. Scranton had done in a place far from her homeland 120 years ago.

As part of its 120th Anniversary, Ewha started the EGPP in Spring 2006 with the goal of enrolling a total of 120 students from developing countries in four years. The EGPP is tangible evidence of the University's strong desire to employ its unique experience and expertise in women education to help women elsewhere in the world to become leaders and effective members of modern society in their respective countries and regions.

Spreading the Spirit of Ewha

The greater involvement of Ewha alumnae in the activities of local alumnae chapters and the International Foundation nurtured a reawakening and strengthening of the Spirit of Ewha among participants. This was accompanied by an increased interest in helping students of Ewha and the development of the University through donations, both small and large. In the early 2000s, the annual number of individual donors approached 300. Additionally, there were 12 or more alumnae chapters and a dozen churches, corporations and foundations which made donations each year.

There are numerous Ewha alumnae living in North America who demonstrate their spirit of Ewha through donations. Some contributions, while perhaps modest in monetary value because of the individual's limited financial resources, are considered especially precious because of their richness in spirit. Other donors, because of their material blessings, are able to show their commitments to Ewha through major donations towards Ewha campus building construction and scholarship endowments. In addition to alumnae donors already mentioned, several more are mentioned here as further representation of the many alumnae donors who have strengthened Ewha with their gifts.

Ms. Young Za Kim, '57 Pharmacy major, contributed $300,000 for the Young Za Kim Scholarship Fund in 2005 (with the promise of another $100,000 being given via annual gifts). She came to South Korea right after 1945 from North Korea. She entered Ewha in 1953. Upon graduation in 1957 she worked at Ewha as a Residence Hall Director. In 1962 she came to New York University and San Francisco State University for graduate study in Nuclear Medicine. She worked as Pharmacist at Kaiser Hospital and invested in real estate. Her mother inspired her with the teaching of *Education for Survival*. Following her mother's teaching, she wanted to help future generations to have the opportunity to attend Ewha. She was elected as a Foundation Board Member in 2005.

Mrs. Kyung Joo Hong Yoon, '59 Pharmacy major, donated $100,000 toward the Ewha Paju Complex Research Fund (later re-designated due to cancellation of the Paju project). She also contributed $100,000 toward the scholarship endowment for pharmacy students who needed financial help. Her appreciation for achieving highest academic achievement recognition by Ewha inspired her to contribute to Ewha. The scholarship endowment was a gift from her husband, Dr. Inbae Yoon, in celebration of her 70th birthday. Mrs. Yoon became a Foundation Board Member in 2007.

Mrs. Sook Hyun Lee, '67 Home Economics major, established a scholarship endowment in 2002. It reached its initial goal of $100,000 in 2006. She promised another $100,000, which is being given in annual gifts. She helped develop the Los Angeles Ewha Alumnae Chapter

Young Za Kim

Kyung Joo Yoon

Sook Hyun Lee

Bok Hyung Lee

Ewha alumnae representative of the many donors for Ewha [International Foundation Archives]

as a leader and had a leadership role to support the Young Music Concert Band in Los Angeles. She has served as a philanthropist for the local community in Los Angeles. Mrs. Lee became a Foundation Board member in 2003.

Mrs. Bok Hyung Lee, '61 Physical Education major who studied Korean traditional dance, established a scholarship for Ewha students studying Korean traditional dance who need financial help. The $100,000 scholarship endowment was a 70th birthday gift from her husband, Mr. Byung Joon Lee. Mrs. Lee became a Foundation Board member in 2007.

The Ewha graduates described above who contributed to the Foundation are a few among many who joined the *River of Faith* to benefit Ewha students and Ewha.

"Gates Are Open to the New World"

The partnership between the Foundation and Ewha goes beyond that of providing financial and other assistance to the University. It is also a partnership engaged in globalizing the role of women to full participation in society in Korea and worldwide. As stated by Kofi Annan, United Nations Secretary-General (5 June 2000):

> *... there is no development strategy more beneficial to society as a whole – women and men alike – than one which involves women as central players. ... the future of this planet depends on women.*

As President of the Foundation, Bishop Sharon Rader, along with Vice President of the Foundation Bishop Ann Sherer-Simpson, and Board Member Dr. Soon-Young Yoon attended the UN Commission on the Status of Women; *Women's Worlds 2005 Congress* (*WW05*)*: 9th International Interdisciplinary Congress on Women* held at Ewha on June 19-24, 2005. It was co-hosted by the Korean Association of Women's

Studies and Ewha Womans University through its Asian Center for Women's Studies. WW05 was the first Congress held in Asia and one of the largest ever with 3,000 participants, including feminist scholars, activists and policy makers from all over the world. Its theme was Embracing the Earth: East-West/North-South.

At the 36th Foundation Annual Board Meeting in November 2005, held at the Marriot Hotel, Warrensville Heights, Ohio, President Rader enthusiastically described the *Women's Worlds 2005 Congress*.

> *Women are making a difference all across the world as they labor in classrooms, courtrooms, hospitals, media, business ... the list could go on and on. The Conference brought freshness of thought and new insights ... the women of Ewha are each one a treasure and sign of the change that is possible in this troubled world of ours. ... Historical events from 108 years ago to the present have brought Koreans and U.S. women together to partner together and continue to grow into responsible and visionary leadership.*

The total assets of the Foundation continued to grow by 2005 to $5,637,969, up from $5,023,053 in 2004. The disbursement for the scholarships for Ewha totaled $176,500 in fiscal year 2006.

In May 2006, at the invitation of Ewha President Shin In-ryung, Foundation President Bishop Sharon Rader and 12 Board members visited Korea to celebrate Ewha's 120th Anniversary. They took part in various celebration events.

The 120th Anniversary Celebration and related events greatly impressed Bishop Rader and the visiting Foundation members. At the 37th Annual Board Meeting of the International Foundation held in November 2006 in Toronto, Canada, Bishop Rader spoke of "The Gates Are Open" as a metaphor to describe happenings at Ewha and the Foundation :

The opening of Ewha's new Front Gate swings wide to welcome students, faculty, and visitors, Seoul, the Korean peninsula and ... around the world ... . Ewha's gates are open toward the new Ewha-Samsung Campus Center to provide an even stronger learning community. The new Ewha Global Partnership Program: the gates have been opened. The sharing that will take place as women of Korea and those from around the world learn, study, and fellowship together will bless not only the students but also the world. ... Floodgates were opened for me and other representatives of this Foundation as we joined with about 50 women students from the University who were recipients of our scholarships. ... Know that your service (via the Foundation) to the women of Ewha is opening the gate of opportunity and hope ... .

At the 37th Annual Meeting, the Foundation was honored to have the new President of Ewha University, Dr. Lee Bae-yong, and University

Foundation President Bishop Rader and Board members with Ewha scholarship recipients [International Foundation Archives]

Ewha's 13th President Lee Bae-yong [Ewha Archives]

faculty and staff members in attendance. As the 13th President of Ewha University, Dr. Lee presented a new vision for Ewha for the next four years. Producing globalized professionals and academia-industry researchers was given high priority, with Ewha being a creative place where progressive and original research thrives. *Initiative Ewha* was introduced to describe the vision that promotes global perspectives and virtues in all Ewhaians. President Lee's intent was to strive to make the Ewha campus a center for different players – from numerous cultural, racial, and political backgrounds. Goals were set to develop integrated international courses and establish global educational infrastructures and networks that would enable 10% of Ewha students to study overseas. Another goal was to build a Paju education and research complex. This would be built in Paju, North Gyeonggi Province by 2010 in preparation for eventual reunification of the Korean peninsula.

A Paju Initiative Fund was initiated by Ewha President Lee with the assistance of vigorous solicitation by Dr. Lee Myungsun, Dean of Publicity and Development, Ewha Womans University. The Office of Development disseminated *Initiative Ewha* material with the Paju Complex as its centerpiece. By 2008, the International Foundation collected $129,000 in contributions for the Paju project. With great disappointment, this project was terminated as of 2011 because of land acquisition problems that raised costs to levels unacceptable to the University. The raised funds were returned to the donors or re-designated by donors for other Ewha purposes. While unsuccessful, the Paju project exemplified Ewha's willingness to accept risk as it aggressively plans forward in creative and visionary ways.

In fiscal year 2008, the International Foundation received $469,595 in contributions. Of the total, $270,850 was applied to scholarships for 69 Ewha students.

Meeting Financial Challenges

At the 39th Annual Board meeting in November 2008, the Foundation faced the same perilous economic times that the U.S., Korea, and the rest of the world were facing.

Vice President Ann B. Sherer-Simpson, substituting for President Sharon Rader, presided over the 39th Annual Board meeting November 2008 at the Bellevue, Washington Hilton Hotel. Bishop Sherer-Simpson offered a meditation on blessing and what it means to be blessed so that we can bless:

> *God calls persons and communities into blessing so that God's great hope for the world could then happen. With regard to Ewha and our Foundation, has not God called us, blessed us, so that we can then rise up and bless others? The calling is not to ease and privilege, but to a life of identifying what is justice, and then calling forth justice. Through us, people all around the world can be blessed.*

Foundation Vice President
Bishop Ann B. Sherer-Simpson
[International Foundation Archives]

Fall 2008 was a time when the overall U.S. economy was in free-fall and potentially bringing on a world-wide depression. For the first time, the net assets of the Foundation dropped because of investment losses, from $6,673,326 in 2007 to $5,887,355 in 2008. Consequently, the Finance Committee notified the International Education and

Cultural Exchange (IE &CE) Committee that no funds were available for scholarships in 2009.

The prospect of sending no scholarship funds to Ewha was disquieting to many at the meeting because substantial scholarship support had been sent every year since 1999. The impact on Ewha at the time it also was suffering bad economic times and most in need of assistance for students was considered to be very serious. The IE&CE Committee, with Board Member Mr. Young Whan Park as Chair, proposed that funds be found elsewhere in the Foundation's assets to send scholarship funds. It was finally resolved by the Board that $100,000 be borrowed from the Reserve Fund and the Mark Gaston Scholarship Fund (with Mr. Gaston's approval) in equal amounts to send $100,000 to Ewha for 40 scholarships in the amount of $2,500 each.

The 40th Annual Board Meeting the following year (November 2009) was in the Englewood, Colorado Inverness Hotel. The Ewha Womans University United Alumnae Chapters of North America held its annual meeting concurrently with the Foundation's meeting hosted by the Denver Alumnae Chapter.

At the Foundation's Annual Meeting, Treasurer Dr. Bumsun Lee, reported that the status of the Foundation's assets had considerably improved since the year before and "We have made good progress in an unstable market, we received about $500,000 for investment and were able to maintain an approximately $6 million portfolio." The report was delivered with a sense of optimism for the future.

Gratitude was expressed to the Investment Sub-Committee members Dr. Bumsun Lee, Mr. Mark Gaston and Dr. Maxwell J. Rhee.

On the occasion of the Foundation's 40 years of dedicated assistance to Ewha Womans University, the Executive Committee advanced a motion presented by the Foundation's Secretary, Dr. Marc Mullinax, calling on the Foundation to set a goal to raise $10 million dollars in the next 10 years. To affirm their strong intentions, the Board members passed the resolution twice.

In recognition of the Foundation's first 40 years while looking forward into the future, the Board set plans for a 40th Anniversary Celebration, which would also launch a new endowment campaign, to be held on April 15, 2010.

The committee members for organizing and conducting the 40th Anniversary event were Board members Dr. Soon-Young Yoon, Dr. Jung Jin Kim El-Mallawany, Rev. Dr. Constance Pak, Mrs. Mee Sang Ahn Chang, Mrs. Sue Konarska, Mr. Mark Gaston, Dr. Hai Won Chang, and Dr. Hwain Chang Lee, and Executive Director Ji-yei Park.

Honoring the Past: The Foundation's 40th Anniversary Celebration

On April 15, 2010, more than one hundred members and friends of the International Foundation gathered at the Ridgewood Country Club in Paramus, New Jersey to celebrate 40 years of the Foundation's commitment and compassion as part of Ewha's *River of Faith*.

The happy celebration was presided over by Dr. Soon-Young Yoon, the Chair of the Committee of Fundraising and Promotion. President Sharon Rader delivered the invocation and welcoming address. She said:

Forty years ago, Dr. Helen Kim and a group of friends from North America gathered to dream a dream – a big dream. They dreamed of a Foundation that would gather resources and funds to provide scholarship assistance, and tell the story of a small but mighty university: Ewha Womans University, a university geared to the needs and hopes of women who would change the country and the world. Those early visionaries gave of their time, their knowledge and their money to assure a strong future for the women of Korea.

Throughout the years, many others have joined in the dream, par-

ticipating in the growth and strengthening of Ewha and the Foundation. More students were enrolled, more faculty was gathered, more buildings were built. A global commitment was introduced – all to bring Ewha to its prominent place in higher education around the world.

Tonight we gather to celebrate the work of the International Foundation for Ewha Womans University and the contributions of so many over the last 40 years. The growth of the University brought additional needs and the Foundation has sought to be responsive. It is with joy that the Foundation welcomes you to this dinner and to the ongoing growth and expansion of support by North Americans for Ewha. ...[50]

As part of the celebration, the Foundation launched the Helen Kim Society as a new avenue for supporting Ewha and its students. Through the Helen Kim Society friends of Ewha, families, graduates of Ewha and other organizations can make financial commitments to the Foundation. These endowments will support Ewha and students for generations.

Bishop Sharon Z. Rader and Dr. Soon-Young Yoon at the International Foundation 40th Anniversary event [International Foundation Archives]

The Society consists of two parts: the Helen Kim Heritage Society includes donors who include Ewha Foundation in their wills, and the Helen Kim Leadership Society includes donors who give over $100,000 towards scholarships. These generous gifts are used to support deserving students in need of financial assistance.

At the 40th Anniversary Celebration, 26 donors were inducted into the Helen Kim Leadership Society for their $100,000 or greater donations to scholarship endowments. Ten donors were in-

Helen Kim Leadership Society donors at the 40th Anniversary of the Foundation
[International Foundation Archives]

ducted into the Helen Kim Heritage Society for contributing to the Foundation through their wills. (Names of Helen Kim Society members appear in Appendix D.)

Helen Kim Society members are awarded the "Alice R. Appenzeller Award" (an honoring certificate), which recognizes the special role of Dr. Alice Appenzeller in the history of Ewha and in early fundraising for Ewha that eventually led to the creation of the International Foundation. With special acknowledgement by the Foundation President, member names are published in the Foundation newsletter and appear on the Foundation's website.

Funds covering the 40th Anniversary Dinner and related costs were generously donated by Drs. William and Hwain Chang Lee.

On the following day, April 16, 2010, Foundation Board members attended the Foundation's Mid-Year Board Meeting and reviewed the 40th Anniversary Celebration. Donations related to the 40th Anniversary gathering totaled $663,525 including pledged gifts. Of special note was the Board's establishment of the Sharon Zimmerman Rader Scholarship

Drs. William and Hwain Chang Lee with Bishop Rader at the International Foundation 40th Anniversary Celebration [International Foundation Archives]

Fund with the undesignated income from the 40th Anniversary Celebration. The newly created endowment honors the love and dedication of Bishop Rader to the Foundation. The Rader Scholarship Fund was set up with a goal of building a $100,000 endowment to generate funds to support non-Korean students from North America to attend the Ewha International Summer College program. Within a year, the funds contributed to the endowment of the Rader Scholarship Fund approached $50,000.

Perhaps a most fitting way of summarizing the International Foundation's first 40 years is through the eyes of someone who was completing his tenure as an intimate and integral participant throughout the organization's existence.

Dr. Bumsun Lee, the Treasurer of the Foundation, made his last financial report to the Foundation at the 41st Annual Board Meeting of the Foundation on October 24, 2010:

Bishop Sharon Rader, Drs. Bumsun and Hyang Won Lee [International Foundation Archives]

I am delighted to see everyone here this morning. I would like to provide you with a brief summary and update of the status of our Fund.

Our more conservative management has offered us good returns in view of the volatile markets that we have experienced as a Nation these past few years. We have been able to maintain our Fund position at over $7 million despite the unstable capital markets.

Our Fund Accounts consist of Cash and Reserve Fund (1.31%), Bonds and Fixed Income Group (59.39%), and Stocks (39.30%).

This will serve as my final report as Treasurer of the Ewha Foundation as I am resigning from my position after today. ...

Forty-three years ago, on her last visit to the United States, Dr. Helen Kim... asked me to serve on the Ewha International Foundation, and to help take care of the funds. I was honored and I accepted this role with a great sense of privilege and responsibility. During the past 40 years the Ewha Foundation has had nine presidents including Bishop Sharon Zimmerman Rader, 181 Board Members including Dr. Hai

Won Chang and Dr. Chang Hyun Shin Geer, and 5 Executive Directors including the Current Director, Mrs. Ji-yei Park. I would like to take this opportunity to thank each of them for their help and guidance over these many years.

During the past 40 years, seven Presidents have served Ewha University including the current President, Dr. Sun-uk Kim. I welcome you here to New York City as you attend our Annual meeting. We salute all of your efforts, leadership, and vision.

With pride, I report to you that the Ewha Foundation received contributions of 10 million dollars during these past 40 years, and has sent 7 million dollars to Ewha in Seoul, Korea. We currently have a balance of 7 million dollars....

I will always treasure the time that I have spent with you, not to mention the many close friendships that have been made along the way. It has truly been an honor and a privilege and a source of endless fond memories. I wish you all the best. May God bless you, the Foundation and Ewha Womans University.

Dr. Bumsun Lee's 40th and final annual report in his own words were repeated here to serve as an example of the dedicated work he and so many others across the generations have made and continue to make to the *River of Faith* of which Ewha Womans University and the International Foundation are part. He did it, he said, because Dr. Helen Kim "asked me to serve ..." and "I was honored and I accepted this role with a great sense of privilege and responsibility."

The Future Outlook

While this book was being written, a new phase of the University was emerging. On August 1, 2010, Ewha Womans University installed Dr. Kim Sun-uk as its 14th President. Dr. Kim studied law as an undergraduate and graduate student at Ewha and earned her doctoral degree in administrative law from the University of Kostnaz in Germany. She has been a professor at Ewha's School of Law since 1995.

Ewha's 14th President Kim Sun-uk
[International Foundation Archives]

President Kim proposed a vision for Ewha as an open academic community which would nurture creative talents equipped with "multi-cultural and multi-lingual capacities and a commitment toward humanization of women at a global level by producing female leaders to play a pivotal role."

In 2011, Ewha Womans University marked its 125th Anniversary by celebrating the education of women in Korea and the world with the theme, "**Ewha, Where Change Begins**."

The stage has been set. The enlightened leadership of Ewha Womans University is imagining the future and taking action. The International Foundation is enthusiastically providing support as Ewha moves forward.

Part 11

Moving Forward

In summary, this study has been an attempt to place the International Foundation for Ewha Womans University within the framework of the larger history of women seeking and achieving greater societal participation, respect, and equality through a unique institution, Ewha Womans University. The search produced a story necessarily incomplete as its beginnings are shrouded by time and the parts about which we have knowledge are mostly through written words and artifacts that can never convey the fullness of their times. However, these fragments of the past and the vivid recollections of those seniors still with us that reach as far back as three-quarters of a century do reveal a very strong, inspiring, and enduring story which Dr. Alice Appenzeller's visualization led this author to succinctly describe as the *River of Faith*.

The *River of Faith* specific to Ewha Womans University and the International Foundation can be traced upstream to a group of women in the northeastern United States in the mid-19th century. American women were involved in foreign mission beginning as early as 1812 by accompanying and supporting their missionary husbands. By mid-century, there were limited numbers of unmarried women being placed in mission, primarily as teachers, to work cooperatively with missionary wives to educate girls and women.

During the same period, there was growing frustration with the dominant policy of the major Protestant mission boards which tightly restricted the role of women in mission. Groups of church women began organizing to form independent mission boards run by women to send single and married women out as missionaries. From the 1860s onward, more than 40 autonomous missionary societies were organized by women in North America. Their common purpose was to send women to minister to the particular needs of women and children, needs which male missionaries could not or did not address. They engaged in direct evangelism, educational and medical missions.

Both Ewha Womans University and the International Foundation had their origins in these 19th century American women's missionary efforts. Specifically, they arose from the work of the Woman's Foreign Missionary Society which was established by women in 1869 under the auspices of the Methodist Episcopal Church. Their efforts became known as *Woman's Work for Woman.*

The foreign mission effort through the *Woman's Work for Woman* movement built a broad membership base of support through collecting two cents a week from members. Of the movement's beginnings, American social reformer Helen Barrett Montgomery (1861-1934) wrote:

> *The women asked for two cents a week, – asked it from door to door; devised mite boxes, formed small local circles, held frequent meetings, looked after children, old women, poor people, hand-picked their own fruit, and astonished the world with their success.*

From such beginnings, the women's missionary societies grew into powerful and effective institutions. The zeal for mission opened frontiers for women everywhere, regardless of whether they were the recipients or deliverers of mission. In the *Woman's Work for Woman* movement, North American women gained leadership skills through the marshaling, managing, and applying of resources as they conducted missions abroad. In countries where missions were sent, including Korea, mission meant that particular needs were being addressed, especially those of women and children deemed of little value in their traditional cultures.

It was the Woman's Foreign Missionary Society, fueled by its expansive membership, that sent women missionaries to many countries. Included were Scranton, Frey, and Appenzeller, who laid the foundations for Ewha and the education and empowerment of Korean women.

Dr. Alice Appenzeller, often with the help of members of Woman's Foreign Missionary Society and friends, sought funds and built a network of supporters through faith and prayers during arduous decades of economic and political turmoil. She had dreams to educate women in Korea in modern buildings similar to those of Wellesley College where she had once been a student. Her undauntable optimism foretold of dreams coming true for women in the impoverished Korean society. She demonstrated her certainty of such an outcome through many actions, exemplified by the realization of Ewha's Sinchon campus through many years of networking, prayers, and hard work. Her fervent prayers with her infectious optimism laid the social network of friends for Ewha.

Other networks of supporters emerged over time, particularly those nurtured by Dr. Helen K. Kim. The ecumenical Ewha Cooperative Board of North America brought together Presbyterians, Methodists, and members of the United Church of Canada and the Australian Presbyterian Church to provide helping hands. In 1951, as the Korean War raged, the World Division of the General Board of Global Ministries of the United Methodist Church formalized the Ewha Womans University Cooperating Board of North America and provided financial assistance to the Ewha

Evacuee Campus in Busan. It later made major contributions to the reconstruction and rehabilitation of Ewha's Seoul campus that was scarred by war.

Establishing the Foundation: University Partnership

During the late 1960s, Korea was facing new challenges of political and economic changes. Dr. Helen Kim, then serving as the Chair of Ewha Womans University Board of Trustees, moved forward with the dream to advance Ewha to a world class university by implementing a fundraising program to update the University hospital and medical college and grow the graduate school component of Ewha.

With great persistence, Dr. Helen K. Kim and friends sought other approaches to fundraising in North America through organizational restructuring. Although she did not live to see its creation, the final step in this transition was the inauguration of the International Foundation for Ewha Womans University, Inc. on April 15, 1970. Mrs. Betty Seabury Hibben (later, Dr. Betty Seabury Mitchell) was elected as the first President.

Helping in Shaping the Future of Ewha

The International Foundation has delivered unique and critical services to Ewha Womans University through financial assistance for the construction of buildings and the support of faculty enhancement, instructional equipment, services of educational programs, and scholarships for students. The contributions have varied depending on needs. At times, such as in the 1970s and 1980s, the Foundation was a linchpin essential to Ewha's rapid growth. One of many unique contributions was major support for the building and equipping of the Centennial Library. The Foundation also facilitated the delivery of books, science laboratory equipment, musical instruments, medical equipment, and contributions for Mokdong Hospital.

From the mid-1980s and onward the Foundation focused on the growth of endowments for scholarships, bolstered by a new investment policy that gave added value to subsequent scholarship disbursements.

One of the preeminent and remarkable commitments has been the assistance of the Seabury Foundation that has supported Ewha professors for academic excellence through faculty enhancement fellowships .

In the mid-1980s, the Foundation began focusing on the growth of the individual endowments for scholarships and other purposes. By 2009, the numbers of such endowments had grown to 159. Funds generated by these endowments flow annually to Ewha, for student scholarships and other purposes.

Strengthening the Partnership with Ewha Alumnae

Forging and strengthening crucial networks among the growing numbers of Ewha alumnae, relatives, and friends in North America, particularly during the 1980s to 1990s, was the emerging reality of the Foundation. Beginning in the late 1960s, local Ewha Alumnae Chapters began forming, by the late 1990s there were about 35 chapters in the United States and Canada.

These chapters became the vital engines for the Foundation to set up scholarship endowments, contributions to the construction and equipping of buildings such as the Centennial Library, renovation of the Welch-Ryang Auditorium, and other support for the growth of the University.

Seeking the New Vision

The supportive international efforts through the Foundation and its predecessor organizations have been and will continue to be integral to Ewha Womans University's evolution to a premier world-class edu-

International Foundation 2010 Annual Meeting with Ewha President Kim Sun-uk (center)
[International Foundation Archives]

cational and research institution. The Foundation has transformed and flourished over time to better meet the needs of the University while recognizing changes in the international donor base, especially the increasing role of Ewha alumnae, relatives, and friends.

It is evident the Foundation has invited new possibilities for support of the University and its students. Over the several decades of existence, the Foundation has seen and responded to the changing needs of Ewha and its students. Presently, the Foundation provides significant numbers of students with support enabling them to take advantage of the exciting educational opportunities the University offers. The Foundation also partners with the University as it develops Ewha for the future.

At the end of the first decade of the 21st century, the Foundation was managing more than 103 scholarship endowments, 26 local alumnae chapter scholarship endowments, and 15 other Foundation funds. Looking forward, the International Foundation can anticipate significant accomplishments in partnership with Ewha Womans University, not only to assist Ewha students but also to provide helping hands as the University promotes women's education globally, and particularly, in developing countries.

Ewha University has grown to more than 21,000 students in 2010 with 188,000 graduates of bachelors, masters, and doctorates since its beginning. The University has 16 colleges: the College of Liberal Arts, the College of Law, the College of Social Sciences, the College of Business Administration, the College of Natural Sciences, the College of Engineer, College of Education, College of Home Economic, the College of Human Ecology, the College of Music, the College of Arts and Design, and the College of Human Movement and Performance, the College of Music, the College of Medicine, the College of Pharmacy, and the College of Nursing. Thirteen graduate schools focus on specific areas, offering Master's degree programs and combined Master's-Doctoral degree programs covering a broad range of disciplines.

Following the *River of Faith* that has carried the contributions and dreams of dedicated people, mostly women, which helped make Ewha Womans University what it is today has truly been an inspirational journey. The International Foundation can be proud of being an important part of that *River of Faith*.

In 2011, Ewha celebrated its 125th Anniversary, with the themes *Ewha, Where Change Begins* and *Share and Serve* for the local community and global community under the leadership of President Kim Sun-uk. The International Foundation for Ewha Womans University is ideally positioned in its partnership with Ewha for even greater opportunities toward building a world in which women fully participate in society to the betterment of all humankind. As Dr. Helen Kim quoted Robert Browning, "The best is yet to be."

There are insights that can be drawn from this remarkable *River of Faith*, the current status and issues facing the Ewha Womans University/International Foundation partnership, and suggestions for future cooperative action.

The *River of Faith* story reveals a multigenerational effort to uplift the status of women to full and equal partners in society. Through their Christian faith and determination, multitudes of women (and many men) have contributed. They have taught us all a very valuable lesson. Everyone can imagine and contribute to a better world through whatever means are available, regardless of the time or circumstance.

The accomplishments of Ewha Womans University and the International Foundation over many years lead to the realization that the present is far from the end of the story. Just as those in the past looked and acted forward from their vantage points in time, those in the present also imagine the future and are acting to strengthen the flow of the *River of Faith*. The need to think forward and take action is as great as ever. The goal of women worldwide becoming full partners in all aspects of society is far from realization.

Ewha Womans University has long recognized its potential as a vehicle for aggressively pursuing inequity wherever it exists, both domestically and internationally, through education and leadership training. Ewha President Chung Ii-sook, at the 16th Annual Board Meeting of the International Foundation in 1985, announced the goal of opening Ewha's doors to the third world through the "... advancement of the status of Ewha from the receiving university to a giving university." With that statement, she was expanding the University's mission based on the premise that the future welfare of Korean women and women everywhere is inextricably linked. In the years since, Ewha embodied this goal in its drive to become a premier world-class university. Evidence of this includes its co-hosting of the UN Commission on the Status of Women's *Women's Worlds 2005 Congress* (*WW05*) by Ewha's Asian Center for Asian Studies and the University's Ewha Global Partnership Program (EGPP).

The International Foundation leadership has recognized this expanded vision of Ewha Womans University. At the Foundation's 37th Annual

Ewha Global Partnership Program students [Ewha Archives]

Board Meeting, President Bishop Sharon Rader spoke glowingly that *The Gates Are Open* at Ewha and the Foundation. She described Ewha's new Front Gate opening wide to welcome others in numerous ways, including the statement, "The sharing that will take place as women of Korea and those from around the world learn, study, and fellowship together will bless not only the students but also the world."

Ewha Womans University is actively demonstrating its intent to reach beyond Korea by sharing Ewha's academic excellence with women from other parts of the world. The University's Ewha Global Partnership Program (EGPP) is an ambitious initiative with the mission of educating underserved students from developing countries. Ewha is going beyond the borders of Korea to unite with the women of the world, many of whom share in common the experience of prejudice and oppression in their home countries. Ewha's goal is to share its achievements and abilities by training professionals and leaders to function in the global arena.

Ewha's EGPP and other international efforts provide opportunities for the International Foundation to view Ewha as far more than the final destination of its assistance. Imagine, in addition to the support it provides to help meet needs on the Ewha campus, the International Foundation works to acquire resources enabling Ewha to educate, enlighten, and empower women wherever oppression of females exists. In true partnership, Ewha and the International Foundation can move forward in both in time and space.

The International Foundation for Ewha Womans University is positioned to utilize a mix of imagination, creativity, and fortitude to assist Ewha Womans University in fulfilling Dr. Helen Kim's dream of internationalism in which all people, including women and regardless of national boundaries, fully participate in society. The International Foundation has the opportunity to spread its wings to not only to benefit Ewha Womans University, but through Ewha, to benefit a much wider audience.

The *River of Faith* does not end at Ewha; the reality is that it grows in depth, breadth, and strength as it flows *through* Ewha.

Epilogue

Searching for and writing a historical perspective of the International Foundation for Ewha University led this author to a feeling of profound gratitude for the courageous trailblazers who helped to shape the future for women in Korea. In a broader sense, my search into the past made me realize more than ever the impact of education on the status of women in Korea and throughout the world.

In search of the history in which the International Foundation is embedded, I discovered a very important part of my own being. I started my journey of history writing because of my gratefulness to Ewha for the education it provided me as well as the confidence it nurtured in me through self-actualization. I have come to realize how much my life (as I am sure have the lives of many others) has been so greatly impacted by what Dr. Alice Appenzeller no doubt would describe as a *River of Faith*.

My awareness of Ewha Womans University came gradually during childhood.

I was born into Chung Dong First Methodist Church in Seoul, where my family had attended for a generation before my arrival into this world. The history of the church and Ewha Haktang were intertwined from their beginnings.

In that church, my faith was shaped and gave me hope to become an educated person. Although I was a child, I was aware of Dr. Helen Kim as she frequently attended Chung Dong Church. From the time I was 10 years old, she inspired me, as she did many young girls, to become a "person." This was radical thinking during my childhood when the norm was that girls and women belonged to men. Part of the inspiration also came from observing my mother (widowed with six children since I, the youngest, was 5 years old) managing to keep her family together through tumultuous years.

I vividly recall seeing and hearing Dr. Alice Appenzeller when she arrived back in Korea in 1947 because of her greetings during Sunday church services. She was tall, handsome, and exuberant. The name of Appenzeller was frequently spoken in our family with admiration, as the church was founded by Dr. Alice Appenzeller's father, Rev. Henry Appenzeller, on October 11, 1885.

During the Korean War and the post war, the Korean economy was devastated. It was also the time when traditions were openly questioned. Among these was the convention that girls were destined to be married to someone chosen by the family, even if they had been fortunate enough to have some education.

Dr. Helen Kim demonstrated that even women can have choices in life and become capable persons with their own identities. I was inspired to go to Ewha to become an educated "person" with a life of choice. I entered Ewha in 1953 and majored in Education. At that time, the University had few material resources and bare facilities. There were few textbooks, so much of the learning was directly from whatever professors lectured or read in the class. However, university life was joyous and hopeful as we could listen to lectures, write papers, and engage in extracurricular activities such as being a University newspaper reporter.

Of special value was involvement in student YWCA activities to receive leadership training and to help others.

Daily chapel service inspired students to be good Christians. At one chapel service, in 1956, Dr. Helen Kim gave a sermon that made a life-long impact on me. It was based on *Matthew 13:31-32*:

> *The kingdom of heaven is like a mustard seed, which a man took and planted in his field. Though it is the smallest of all your seeds, yet when it grows, it is the largest of garden plants and becomes a tree that the birds of the air come and perch in its branches.*

In so many ways, Ewha provided me with the opening to the rest of my life. I will always be indebted because of its gifts to me.

Chang Hyun Shin Geer (신장현)

Appendices

Appendix A

Dr. Helen Kim's Last Words

I do believe in the immortality of the human soul; and I have lived my daily life seeking God's strength in order to obtain a better way of life in obedience to His will. Trying to overcome physical and other limitations, I have strived always to walk a victorious path in my own way.

I do not believe that I die when the function of my earthly body becomes weak and my heart beat stops. I do not want to be treated as dead just because my body has returned to the earth. Instead of a funeral, if my relatives, friends, and colleagues want it, I hope they will give me a farewell service sending me away to the glorious path of victory and blessed life which I have experienced all through my life. I want the service rather to be a magnificent and exciting concert filled with songs of victory, glory and life.

I am leaving behind me a great debt of love which I owe to my parents, brothers and sisters, and to many friends, colleagues and teachers in the East and the West. I have always known even while I was with you physically that there was and will be no way of repaying all those debts to you. But now I promise that I will love each one of you more than ever. I know very well that our heavenly Father will grant me the future with life more abundant and love overflowing.

To those who did not understand me for any reason, I promise that I shall pray with deeper love and concern for their success in life.

Appendix B

International Foundation Board Founding Members

Mrs. J. A. Barclay
Miss Peggy Billings
Dr. Hai Won Chang
Mrs. C. C. Choi
Dr. Myung Soon Oh
Mrs. F. M. Faist
Mrs. Mowat Fraser
Mrs. Frances Fulton
Mrs. E. L. Hillman
Mrs. Maude Jensen
Mrs. Bessie Kim
Dr. Okgill Kim
Mr. Edward Poitras
Dr. Samuel Smith
Mrs. Charles Tillett
Dr. Hiram Weld
Dr. Kilchai Yim
Bishop James Armstrong
Mrs. Katherine Sears
Dr. Marie Finger Bale
Dr. Thomas Bennet
Dr. Everlyn Berry
Miss Margaret Billingsley
Mrs. Frank G. Brocks
Mr. E. Frank Carey
Miss Margaret Forsyth
Mr. George Hergesheimer
Dr. George Jarman
Mr. Sae Sun Kim
Mrs. Wayne Lamb
Dr. James Laney
Mrs. James Laney
Mrs. W. Earl Ledden
Mr. P. William Lee
Miss Florence Little
Mrs. W. W. McLendon
Mrs. Gladys Nayor
Mrs. John Norris
Mrs. Henry Oh
Mr. Rymond King
Mrs. S. E. McCreless
Miss Erna Slagg

Appendix C

Concurrent International Foundation and Ewha Presidents

Year	Foundation President	Ewha University President
1970	Peggy Billings (Inaugural Chair)	Kim Okgill
1971	Betty S. Mitchell	Kim Okgill
1972	Betty S. Mitchell	Kim Okgill
1973	Betty S. Mitchell	Kim Okgill
1974	Betty S. Mitchell	Kim Okgill
1975	Betty S. Mitchell	Kim Okgill
1976	Betty S. Mitchell	Kim Okgill
1977	Betty S. Mitchell	Kim Okgill
1978	Betty S. Mitchell	Kim Okgill
1979	Kathryne B. Sears	Chung Ii-sook
1980	Kathryne B. Sears	Chung Ii-sook
1981	Mamie Lee Finger	Chung Ii-sook
1982	Mamie Lee Finger	Chung Ii-sook
1983	Mamie Lee Finger	Chung Ii-sook
1984	Mamie Lee Finger	Chung Ii-sook
1985	Mamie Lee Finger	Chung Ii-sook
1986	Mamie Lee Finger	Chung Ii-sook
1987	Susan Ruby Lamb	Chung Ii-sook
1988	Susan Ruby Lamb	Chung Ii-sook
1989	Julia K. Wilke	Chung Ii-sook
1990	Julia K. Wilke	Yoon Hoo-jung
1991	Julia K. Wilke	Yoon Hoo-jung
1992	Julia K. Wilke	Yoon Hoo-jung
1993	Julia K. Wilke	Yoon Hoo-jung

1994	Julia K. Wilke	Yoon Hoo-jung
1995	Julia K. Wilke	Yoon Hoo-jung
1996	Susanne L. Stevens	Chang Sang
1997	Susanne L. Stevens	Chang Sang
1998	Susanne L. Stevens	Chang Sang
1999	Susanne L. Stevens	Chang Sang
2000	Hannah C. Meadors	Chang Sang
2001	Hannah C. Meadors	Chang Sang
2002	Hannah C. Meadors	Shin In-ryung
2003	Bishop Sharon Z. Rader	Shin In-ryung
2004	Bishop Sharon Z. Rader	Shin In-ryung
2005	Bishop Sharon Z. Rader	Shin In-ryung
2006	Bishop Sharon Z. Rader	Lee Bae-yong
2007	Bishop Sharon Z. Rader	Lee Bae-yong
2008	Bishop Sharon Z. Rader	Lee Bae-yong
2009	Bishop Sharon Z. Rader	Lee Bae-yong
2010	Bishop Sharon Z. Rader	Kim Sun-uk
2011	Bishop Sharon Z. Rader	Kim Sun-uk
2012	Bishop Sharon Z. Rader	Kim Sun-uk

Appendix D

Helen Kim Society

Helen Kim Leadership Society (2012)

Drs. Hai Won Chang & Soon Man Rhim Scholarship
Heeyul Lee Cho Scholarship
Barbara Eunok Yang Choi Scholarship
Myung Sook Ha Chung Scholarship
Myung Soon Woo Chung Scholarship
Dr. Chang Hyun Shin Geer Scholarship
Yaun Dahm Yoo Han Scholarship
Hong, Kyung Joo Scholarship
Sunwha Hong Scholarship
Marian Sharrocks Intemann Memorial Scholarship (Mrs. Suzanne Nelson)
Choon-Hi Choi Kahng Memorial Scholarship (Rev. Raymond Kahng & Children)
Shin Hyung Kim Memorial Scholarship (Dr. John Young Song Kim)
Young Za Kim Scholarship
Gary & Seungsoon Konarska Scholarship
Drs. Bumsun & Hyang Won Lee Medical Scholarship
Byung Joon & Bok Hyung Lee Scholarship
Hwain Chang Lee Scholarship
P. William Lee Scholarship
Sook Hyun Lee Scholarship
Dr. Young Mo & Mrs. Sang Yeon Kim Lee Scholarship
Dr. Young-hee Lowe Scholarship
Jung Hwa Lee Park Scholarship
Drs. Moonja Chung & Chanjong Park Medical Fund
Dr. Young Sook Park Medical Research Fund (Dr. Philip McGann)

Hak He Rhee & Chong Soo Pyun Scholarship
Kilchai K. Yim Endowment for Administration
Kilchai K. Yim Scholarship
Chicago Alumnae Association Scholarship
Medical School Research (Medical School Alumnae Association)
New York Alumnae Association Scholarship
Northern California (San Francisco) Alumnae Association Scholarship
Southern California Alumnae Association Scholarship
Alumnae Association of Greater Washington Scholarship
Detroit Alumnae Scholarship
Houston Alumnae Scholarship

Helen Kim Heritage Society (2012)

Dr. Hai Won Chang
Mrs. Meesang Ahn Chang
Drs. Ira & Chang Hyun Shin Geer
Dr. John Young Song Kim
Dr. Jong H. Lee
Drs. William & Hwain Lee
Mr. Richard Smith & Dr. Soon-Young Yoon
Drs. Amin & Jung Jin Kim El-Mallawany

Notes

1. Frances J. Baker, *The Story of the Woman's Foreign Missionary Society of the Methodist Episcopal Church* (Cincinnati, OH: Cranston & Curts, 1896), 342.
2. Ibid., Frontispiece.
3. Ibid., 342.
4. Dana L. Robert, *American Women in Mission* (Wiley-Blackwell, 2009), 125-188.
5. Choong Ryang Chung, *History of Ewha Eighty Years* (Ewha Womans University Press, 1968), 32-33.
6. Chun Suk Oh, *Han Guk Gyo Yuk Sa* (*History of New Education in Korea*), (Hyun Dae Gyo Yuk Publication, 1964).
7. Frances J. Baker, *The Story of the Woman's Foreign Missionary Society of the Methodist Episcopal Church* (Cincinnati, OH: Cranston & Curts, 1896), 342-343.
8. Dana L. Robert, *American Women in Mission* (Wiley-Blackwell, 2009), 410-415.
9. Chun Suk Oh, *Han Guk Gyo Yuk Sa* (*History of New Education in Korea*), (Hyun Dae Gyo Yuk Publication, 1964), 196-225.
10. Wellesley 125th Anniversary, Person of the Week, October 2, 2000.
11. Choong Ryang Chung, *History of Ewha Eighty Years* (Ewha Womans University Press, 1968), 199-200.
12. Alice R. Appenzeller, Copy of letter written by Alice R. Appenzeller provided by Moon Pyo Hong.
13. Dana Robert, *American Women in Mission* (Wiley-Blackwell, 2009), 288.
14. Choong Ryang Chung, *History of Ewha Eighty Years* (Ewha Womans University Press, 1968), 209.
15. Kyung Lim Shin Lee, *Pear Blossoms Blooming* (Ewha Womans University Press, 1989), 66.
16. Ewha Womans University Archives (Ed.), *Ewha Old and New: 110 Years of History 1886-1996* (Ewha Womans University Press, 2005), 71.
17. Ibid., 75.
18. Choong Ryang Chung, *History of Ewha Eighty Years* (Ewha Womans University Press, 1968), 242-243.
19. Heung Keun Ham (Ed.), *The 100 Years of Ewha Historical Documents and Artifacts* (Ewha Womans University Press, 1994), 118.
20. Ibid., 118.
21. International Foundation for Ewha Womans University, *Ewha News*, Vol. XIV, No. 2, Summer, 1994.
22. Ewha Womans University Archives (Ed.), *Ewha Old and New: 110 Years of History 1886-1996* (Ewha Womans University Press, 2005), 75.
23. Helen Kim, *Grace Sufficient: The Story of Helen Kim* (Nashville, TN: The Upper Room, 1964), 75.

24. Ibid., 95.

25. Ewha Womans University Archives (Ed.), *Ewha Old and New: 110 Years of History 1886-1996* (Ewha Womans University Press, 2005), 75-76.

26. Helen Kim, *Grace Sufficient: The Story of Helen Kim* (Nashville, TN: The Upper Room, 1964), 120.

27. Ewha Cooperating Board in North America, *Minutes of Annual Meeting*, September 13, 1948.

28. Ewha Cooperating Board in North America, *Minutes of Annual Meeting*, May 10-11, 1950.

29. Ewha Cooperating Board in North America, *Minutes of Annual Meeting*, November 15, 1956.

30. Cheonsik Woo, "Upgrading Higher Education in Korea: Context and Policy Response" (Korea Development Institute, December 31, 2002), 8-9.

31. Burnice Jarmen, *The Methodist Women*, December, 1963 issue.

32. Choong Ryang Chung, *History of Ewha Eighty Years* (Ewha Womans University Press, 1968), 415.

33. Letter to Ewha Cooperating Board Members from President Estelle Hillman, August 30, 1967.

34. Ewha Cooperating Board in North America, *Minutes of Annual Meeting*, April 14, 1970.

35. International Foundation for Ewha Womans University, *Minutes of Inaugural Meeting*, April 15, 1970.

36. Ibid.

37. Peggy Billings, *Ewha Foundation 40th Anniversary*, "My Reflections on Dr. Helen Kim and the International Foundation for Ewha Womans University", *Ewha Foundation News*, Vol. XXVIII, Summer, 2010.

38. Ewha Womans University Archives (Ed.), *Ewha Old and New: 110 Years of History 1886-1996* (Ewha Womans University Press, 2005), 112.

39. International Foundation for Ewha Womans University, *Ewha Centennial News*, Winter, 1986.

40. International Foundation for Ewha Womans University, *Minutes of Annual Meeting*, 1986.

41. International Foundation for Ewha Womans University, *Minutes of Annual Meeting*, 1987.

42. International Foundation for Ewha Womans University, *Ewha News*, Vol. VII, No. 1, Winter, 1988.

43. International Foundation for Ewha Womans University, *Ewha News*, Vol. VIII, No. 1, Winter, 1989.

44. International Foundation for Ewha Womans University, *Minutes of Annual Meeting*, 1990.

45. International Foundation for Ewha Womans University, "Ewha in the 21st Century", *Ewha News*, Vol. XV, No.1, Winter, 1995.

46. International Foundation for Ewha Womans University, *Ewha News*, Vol. XIII, Winter, 1994.

47. International Foundation for Ewha Womans University, *Ewha News*, Vol. XIII, Winter, 1994.

48. International Foundation for Ewha Womans University, *Minutes of Inaugural Meeting*, April 15, 1970.

49. Sang Chang, "Excerpts from Annual Report from Ewha Womans University", *Minutes of Annual Meeting*, November 2, 1996.

50. Sharon Z. Rader, International Foundation for Ewha Womans University, *40th Celebration Program*, April 15, 2010.

Selected Bibliography

Archives, Board Meeting Minutes, and Reports

Board of Directors Meeting of the International Foundation, "Minutes of the Inaugural Meeting", April 15, 1970.

Board of Directors of the International Foundation, "Minutes of the First Annual Meeting of the Board of Directors, International Foundation for Ewha Womans University, Inc.", May 5-6, 1971.

Chung, Ii-sook, "President's Address", International Foundation Board Annual Meeting, Washington, DC., November 4, 1995.

Editors of Ewha Photo Diary for the 100th Anniversary of Helen Kim, 1999 Ewha Photo Diary, October 20, 1998.

Ewha Foundation News: *40th Anniversary*, Vol. XXVVIII, Summer, 2010.

Ewha Womans University Archives, Print and Photo, Ewha Womans University.

Finger, Mamie Lee, "President's Annual Report", International Foundation Annual Meeting, November, 1981, November, 1982.

Hillman, Estelle, "Letter to Ewha Cooperating Board Members", August 30, 1967.

International Foundation for Ewha Womans University, *Ewha Centennial News, Ewha News, Ewha Foundation News*, 1982-2011.

International Foundation for Ewha Womans University, *Minutes of Board of Directors Annual Meeting*, 1971- 2011.

Jarman, Burnice H., *Ewha Womans University, A Self-study* (Reprinted from *The Methodist Woman*), December, 1962.

Lamb, Ruby, "President's Annual Report", International Foundation Annual Meeting, November, 1987, November, 1988.

Meadors, Hannah C., "President's Annual Repot", International Foundation Annual Meeting, November, 2000.

"Minutes of the International Foundation of Ewha Womans University Advisory Committee Meeting", January 5, 1971.

Mitchell, Betty S., "President's Annual Report", International Foundation Annual Meeting, November, 1973-1976.

Rader, Bishop Sharon Z., "President's Annual Report", International Foundation Annual Meeting, November, 2003-2011.

Sears, Kathryn B., "President's Annual Report", International Foundation Annual Meeting, November, 1980.

Stevens, Susanne L., "President's Annual Report", International Foundation Annual Meeting, November, 1996-1999.

Wilke, Julia K., "President's Annual Report", International Foundation Annual Meeting,

November, 1989-1995.

Woo, Cheonsik, "Upgrading Higher Education in Korea: Context and Policy Response", Korea Development Institute, December 31, 2002.

Books

Baker, Frances J., *The Story of the Woman's Foreign Missionary Society of the Methodist Episcopal Church*, Cincinnati, OH: Cranston & Curts, 1896.

Bang, H., *Japan's Colonial Educational Policy in Korea 1905-1930*, Ann Arbor, MI: University Microfilm, 1972.

Choi, Min Sook (Ed.)., *Ewha 110 Years of History: Beginning of the Second Century of Ewha 1987-1996*, Seoul, Korea: Ewha Womans University Press, 2006.

Chung, Choong Ryang, *Ewha Palsip Nyeon Sa* (*History of Ewha Eighty Years*), Seoul, Korea: Ewha Womans University Press, 1968.

Chung, Sei-wha (Ed.), Chang Hyun Shin (Geer) et. al. (Trans.), *Challenges for Women: Women's Studies in Korea*, Korean Women's Institute Series, Seoul, Korea: Ewha Womans University Press, 1986.

Ewha Baek Nyeon Sa Pyeon Chan Wi Won Hoe (The Editing Committee of Ewha Centennial History), *Ehwa Baek Nyeon Sa* (*The 100 Years History of Ewha*), Seoul, Korea: Ewha Womans University Press, 1994.

Ewha Womans University Archives (Ed.), *Dr. Helen Kim and Modern Women's Education in Korea: An Illustrated Record Celebration of the 100th Anniversary of Her Birth*, Seoul, Korea: Ewha Womans University Press, 1999.

Ewha Womans University Archives (Ed.), *Ewha Old and New: 110 Years of History 1886-1996*, Seoul, Korea: Ewha Womans University Press, 2005.

Ham, Heung Keun (Chair of Editors), *Ewha Baek Nyeon Sa* (*The 100 Years History of Ewha*), Seoul, Korea: Ewha Womans University Press, 1994.

Ham, Heung Keun (Chair of Editors), *Ewha Baek Nyeon Sa Ja Ryo Jip* (*The 100 Years of Ewha Historical Documents and Artifacts*). Seoul, Korea: Ewha Womans University Press, 1994.

Hong, Yi-sup, *Korea's Self-Identity*, Seoul, Korea: Yonsei University Press, 1973.

International Foundation for Ewha Womans University, *Handbook of the International Foundation for Ewha Womans University*, New York: International Foundation for Ewha Womans University, Inc., 2009.

Kim, Helen, *Grace Sufficient: The Story of Helen Kim*, Nashville, TN: The Upper Room, 1964.

Kim, Helen, *Geu Bit Sok Ui Jak Eun Saeng Myeong* (*A Small Life in the Light: Autobiography of Helen Kim*), Seoul, Korea: Ewha Womans University Press, 1983.

Ku, Daeyeol (Ed.), *1999 Ewha Photo Diary: Light of Women, Helen Kim 1899-1999*, Seoul, Korea: Ewha Womans University Press, 1999.

Lee, Ki-baik, *A New History of Korea*, Edward W. Wagner with Edward J. Shultz (Trans.), Cambridge, MA: Harvard University Press, 1984.

Lee, Kyung Lim Shin, *Pear Blossoms Blooming: History of American Missionaries at Ewha Womans University*, Seoul, Korea: Ewha Womans University Press, 1989.

Oh, Chun Suk, *Han Guk Gyo Yuk Sa* (*History of New Education in Korea*), Seoul, Korea: Hyun Dae Gyo Yuk Publication, 1964.

Oh, John Kie-Chang, *Korean Politics: The Quest for Democratization and Economic Develepement*, Ithaca, NY: Cornell University Press, 1999.

Robert, Dana L., *American Women in Mission: A Social History of Their Thought and Practice*, Macon, GA: Mercer University Press, 2005.

Robert, Dana L., *Christian Mission: How Christianity Became a World Religion*, Chichester, West Sussex, UK: Wiley-Blackwell, 2009.

Son, In-soo, *History of Modern Education in Korea*, Seoul, Korea: Yonsei University Press,1971.

Willoughby, Heather A. (Ed.), *Footsteps Across the Frontier: 120 Years of Globalization at Ewha Womans University*, Seoul, Korea: Ewha Womans University Press, 2007.

Wright, Edward R. (Ed.), *Korean Politics in Transition*, Seattle, WA: University of Washington Press, 1975.

Index

Names

Subjects

--- to enlighten, educate, empower women in Korea and worldwide ---

IFEWU

International Foundation for
Ewha Womans University, Inc.
475 Riverside Drive, Room 1505
New York, N.Y. 10115
www.ewhafoundation.org